Performance-Based
STEM Projects

10

Performance-Based
STEM Projects

Todd Stanley

PRUFROCK PRESS INC.
WACO, TEXAS

Edited by Katy McDowall

Cover and layout design by Allegra Denbo

ISBN-13: 978-1-61821-800-1

Prufrock Press Inc.
P.O. Box 8813
Waco, TX 76714-8813
Phone: (800) 998-2208
Fax: (800) 240-0333
http://www.prufrock.com

TABLE OF CONTENTS

INTRODUCTION   **1**

Why Project-Based Learning?   1

Why STEM?   5

Why STEM and PBL?   7

How This Book Is Organized   8

Project 1: Communicate Effectively   **11**

Project Outline: Create Your Own Crayon   14

Suggested Timeline   15

Lesson: What Are Primary Colors?   16

Lesson: What Are Secondary Colors?   17

Lesson: What Is a "Good" Color?   18

Lesson: How to Develop a Pitch   19

Handout   20

Product Rubric   21

Project 2: Focus on Inquiry and Collaboration   **23**

Project Outline: Art Bot   26

Suggested Timeline   27

Lesson: What Is "Good" Art?   28

Lesson: How to Analyze Art   29

Handouts   31

Project 3: Understand Multiple Content Areas   **35**

Project Outline: Bubblegum   38

Suggested Timeline   39

Lesson: How Many Gumballs Are in the Jar?   40

Lesson: The Social Responsibility of Chewing Gum   41

Lesson: Which Gum Lasts the Longest?   42

Lesson: Expressing Gum Through Poetry   43

Handouts   44

Product Rubric   50

Project 4: Explore Contemporary Issues   **51**

Project Outline: Recycling, Huh! What Is It Good For?   54

Suggested Timeline   55

Lesson: What Is Recycling?   56

Lesson: What Is Recyclable?   57

Lesson: What Are the Benefits of Recycling?   58

Product Rubric   59

Project 5: Use Technology, Math, and Reasoning   **61**

Project Outline: Crack the Code   64

Suggested Timeline   65

Lesson: How Can Numbers Represent Other Things?   66

Lesson: How Do You Create a Code?   67

Handouts   68

Product Rubric   71

Project 6: Use and Analyze Models   **73**

Project Outline: Where in the World Is Your Neighborhood?   76

Suggested Timeline   77

Lesson: How Well Do You Know Your Neighborhood?   78

Lesson: What Are the Different Types of Maps?   79

Lesson: What Makes a Map Look Professional?   80

Handout   81

Product Rubric   83

Project 7: Record and Analyze Data   **85**

Project Outline: How Far Will It Fly?   88

Suggested Timeline   89

Lesson: Setting Up the Experiment   90

Lesson: What Is a Variable?   91

Lesson: Graphing Data   92

Handouts   93

Product Rubric   96

Project 8: Investigate Change Over Time and Patterns   **97**
Project Outline: What Do You See in the Clouds?   100
Suggested Timeline   101
Lesson: What Are Clouds?   102
Product Rubric   103

Project 9: Use Computer Models or Simulations   **105**
Project Outline: What If There Were No Light Bulb?   108
Suggested Timeline   109
Lesson: What Are the Most Important Inventions Ever?   110
Lesson: What Would Life Look Like If
   We Took Away the Light Bulb?   111
Handout   112
Product Rubric   114

Project 10: Construct and Explain Systems   **115**
Project Outline: Everyone Is Playing It   117
Suggested Timeline   118
Lesson: How Are Sports Organized?   119
Lesson: How Is Math Used in Sports?   120
Handout   121
Product Rubric   122

DEVELOP YOUR OWN STEM PROJECTS   **123**

REFERENCES   **129**

ABOUT THE AUTHOR   **131**

NEXT GENERATION SCIENCE STANDARDS ALIGNMENT   **133**

COMMON CORE STATE STANDARDS ALIGNMENT   **135**

INTRODUCTION

Why Project-Based Learning?

When my assistant principal, Dr. Jones, would visit my science and social studies class and observe the project-based learning (PBL) my students were engaged in, he would always ask in the post-conference, "How do you know it is working?" To me, this seemed like asking someone why water is wet. It just is. Through the day-to-day observations, I could see that my students were more engaged and learning more through project-based learning than the traditional teaching methods I had used during the first 5 years of my teaching career. Were their test results better at the end of the year? Yes, but more important than this quantitative data was the qualitative data my students provided me. My students would come to visit me after having left for high school and say, "High school is easy because we used project learning in your class. I knew how to research, I knew how to present, and I remembered the material we learned." When students and their parents would talk about their later schooling experiences, they were always grateful we had done project-based learning because it better prepared them for the future.

Despite these stories, Dr. Jones would always resist: "Where's the research to back up that this is working in the classroom?" This was right at the beginning of the data explosion in education, and I did not have any research to tell me it was working. I just *knew* it was working. Again, Dr. Jones would challenge me: "If you had research to back this up, it would make the power of its effectiveness much better because it would be quantifiable."

Since these conversations, project-based learning has been slowly but surely making its way into the educational conversation. Documentaries such as *Most Likely to Succeed* (Dintersmith & Whiteley, 2015) show the power PBL can have on students. As PBL has gained traction in schools, there has been more and more research on its effectiveness. Not only did I know it was working, but I could also back it up with study after study.

How Effective Is Project-Based Learning?

When Thomas (2000) reviewed research on PBL, he found evidence that using it in the classroom enhanced the quality of student learning, especially when compared to other methods of instruction. Specifically, he saw that PBL was effective for teaching processes, such as problem solving and decision making. Boaler (2002) looked at two British secondary schools that had a similar student makeup. One of these schools used traditional methods to teach mathematics. The other focused on project-based learning. Across 3 years of data, students in the project-based learning school outperformed the traditional school's students in mathematics, with 3 times as many students scoring the highest possible grade on the national examination (Boaler, p. 16). More than that, PBL better taught conceptual and applied knowledge, meaning there was a much better chance of enduring understanding.

In a more recent study, Deitering (2016) looked at whether project-based learning was a more effective instructional method than traditional teaching methods. She compared two groups, one taught through PBL and one taught through more traditional methods. Figure 1 summarizes her findings. Each group completed a science unit on rocks and erosion, followed by a reflection, which required students to consider three levels of engagement—retreatism, compliance, and engagement. The results of the student surveys showed that traditional instruction resulted in better student compliance. When students sit in perfectly positioned rows and are talked *at* for great lengths, it only makes sense that they would be compliant. Traditional methods were also higher in retreatism, but this is not a good thing. Retreatism is when students are disengaged from current classroom activities and goals. Although they are compliant, they are thinking about other things, causing them to reject both the official goals

	Controlled Group Traditional Instruction	Experienced Group PBL Instruction
Retreatism	7%	2%
Compliance	24%	11%
Engagement	44%	82%

FIGURE 1. Traditional instruction versus project-based learning in the classroom and student-reported levels of engagement (Deitering, 2016).

and the official means of achieving the goals of the classroom. When it comes to engagement, PBL wins by a bunch. Eighty-two percent of students said PBL methods were engaging to them, while less than half said the same thing about traditional classroom methods. When you add it all up, compliance may be nice, but it does not mean students are learning.

The Buck Institute for Education (n.d.), which is one of the biggest proponents of PBL, has found that:

- ▸ **PBL engages hearts and minds:** Through active engagement, PBL provides real-world relevance for learning, as students solve problems that are important to them and their communities.
- ▸ **PBL provides deeper learning:** PBL builds deeper understanding and retention.
- ▸ **PBL provides exposure to adults and careers:** Students can interact with mentors in their communities and develop career interests.
- ▸ **PBL provides a sense of purpose:** Seeing the real-world impact of a project gives students a greater sense of purpose.
- ▸ **PBL builds 21st-century workplace skills:** Students learn to take initiative and responsibility, solve problems, and communicate ideas.
- ▸ **PBL provides rewarding teacher-student relationships:** Teachers, too, discover meaning and rediscover the joy of learning while working with students engaged in PBL.
- ▸ **PBL engages creativity and technology:** Students use a variety of approaches and technology tools throughout the course of their projects.

What Is Effective Project-Based Learning?

A literature review by MDRC (Condliffe, 2017) described PBL as "promising but not proven" (p. iii). Notably, however, Condliffe did not find overwhelming evidence of PBL's effectiveness. This is because not all PBL is created equally. Just because someone claims to be "doing PBL" in his or her classroom does not mean he or she is doing so with the best practices in mind (p. 20). There are certain elements needed for effective PBL, including (Menzies, Hewitt, Kokotsaki, Collyer, & Wiggins, 2016):

1. Student support: pupils need to be effectively guided and supported through the PBL process; emphasis should be given on effective time management and student self- management including making safe and productive use of technological resources.
2. Teacher support: regular support needs to be offered to teachers through regular networking and professional development opportunities. Support from the school senior management is crucial.
3. Effective group work: high quality group work will help ensure that pupils share equal levels of agency and participation.
4. Balancing didactic instruction with independent inquiry will ensure that pupils develop a certain level of knowledge and skills allowing them to comfortably engage in independent work.
5. Assessment emphasis on reflection, self, and peer evaluation: evidence of progress needs to be regularly monitored and recorded.
6. An element of student choice and autonomy throughout the PBL process will help pupils develop a sense of ownership and control over their learning. (pp. 10–11)

These elements all need to be in play as you utilize project-based learning in the classroom. As you dive into the projects in this book, you will find they are well laid out for you, but there are certain things that you will have to independently ensure are accomplished, such as managing students, giving them enough space to learn how to learn, and giving them guidance on how to reflect upon what they have learned (Stanley, 2015).

When all is said and done, I know my students are learning much more in my project-based learning classroom than when I was teaching with traditional methods. And now I have the research to back that up. How do you like that, Dr. Jones?

Why STEM?

STEM (science, technology, engineering, and math) education is much more than the mashing together of these subject areas. In this book, students will utilize STEM principles to engage in project-based learning through performance-based projects. These projects will involve:

- Designing, developing, and utilizing technological systems
- Open-ended, problem-based design activities
- Cognitive, manipulative, and effective learning strategies
- Applying technological knowledge and processes to real world experiences using up-to-date resources
- Working individually as well as in a team to solve problems (International Technology and Engineering Educators Association, 2016, para. 3)

Typically, students utilizing STEM principles to engage in PBL will:

- Access and synthesize prior knowledge in science, math, and technology to solve a real-world problem
- Research and collect evidence to solve a problem
- Gain firsthand experience on how science, math, and technology solve problems in the real world
- Conceptualize, build, and test concrete models of solutions
- Work collaboratively to critique and build on their peers' ideas
- Communicate and defend solutions based on evidence (Advancement Courses, 2015, para. 3)

STEM-based PBL provides students with authentic learning experiences. Through such experiences, students understand the context of how what they are learning fits into the real world. This means that students are better equipped to apply a concept or skill in a later project or unit, as well as when they go on to college or enter the workforce. By developing authentic products and solving real-world problems, students are able to experience and see firsthand how classroom concepts work in real-world settings. By utilizing STEM principles, they are also able to see how concepts connect across subject areas.

Traditionally, students might work on math for 45 minutes. Then, the bell rings, and the math books and work go away, only to be replaced by science books and assignments. When the bell rings again, everything students have been learning about is put on hold, and they transition into learning about something else. This is a very unnatural way to learn about science and math—and any other subject, for that matter. Math and science are subject areas that are very close cousins, with a lot of overlap between the two of them. Why do we try so hard to separate them?

Anyone who lives in the real world knows this is not how it works. Oftentimes, you employ several different areas of learning while working on a single project. For example, the simple act of making dinner uses several disciplines:

- ▶ **English language arts:** Reading the recipe or the directions for preparing the meal.
- ▶ **Math:** Measuring out what is needed to create the meal and using a timer to determine how long it should cook.
- ▶ **Science:** Understanding when water is boiling, an oven is warmed, or what to mix and what not to mix together to get the desired results.

By completing almost any task, you integrate different subject areas to be able to achieve a goal. That is the way our lives work, and it is how classrooms should work as well. If the STEM education initiative has done anything, it has taught teachers and students how all of these areas work together and how they can be used collectively to achieve a greater accomplishment than if using a single subject area.

You can also use STEM-based PBL to engage students in the engineering design process (Engineering is Elementary, 2018). See Figure 2 for a breakdown of the process. This five-step cycle (ask, imagine, plan, create, improve) is the same process real-world engineers utilize. This is a sound process that can even be applied to subjects unrelated to science, technology, engineering, or math.

For example, if you have asked students to write an essay on what their favorite color is, they could easily go through these steps in order to complete their task:

- ▶ **Ask:** Students ask and consider, "What is my favorite color?"
- ▶ **Imagine:** Students ask and consider, "Why is it my favorite color?"
- ▶ **Plan:** Students ask and consider, "How could I explain to others why it is my favorite color, and what examples could I use?"
- ▶ **Create:** Students write their essays.
- ▶ **Improve:** Students read through their essays, looking for clarity, as well as spelling and grammar errors.

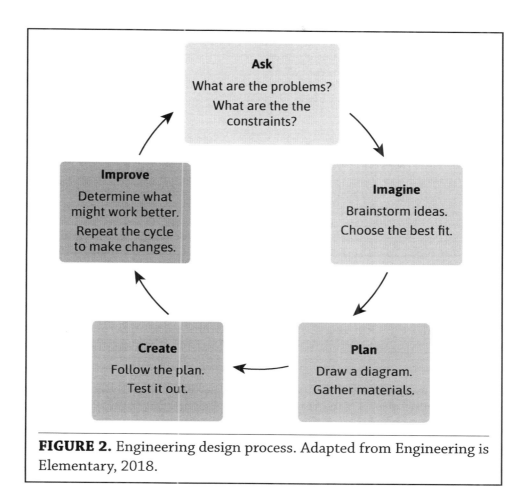

FIGURE 2. Engineering design process. Adapted from Engineering is Elementary, 2018.

The engineering design process gives students a good, solid model to follow, which can be applied throughout STEM areas, as well as to social studies, art, and even gym class. Once students are familiar with the engineering design process, they will intrinsically revert to it whenever they are working on something. This is the true value of STEM learning.

Why STEM and PBL?

STEM-based PBL naturally lends itself to the formation of 21st-century skills, which are crucial to students' development in school and beyond. STEM learning engages students and equips them with critical thinking, problem solving, creative, and collaborative skills. Because of the authentic nature of STEM-based PBL experiences and the final products that students create, students also develop communication skills as well as self-direction. STEM and PBL create a perfect marriage in ensuring students are ready to be the leaders of tomorrow.

How This Book Is Organized

This book features 10 projects. Each project is linked to national STEM education goals. In selecting projects and the skills that they emphasize, I utilized the STEM Learning Goals and the System Dynamics and Systems Thinking Tools and Learning Strategies that make up effective STEM education, according to Creative Learning Exchange (2016; see Figure 3), as a framework. Projects are also based on and aligned to the Next Generation Science Standards and the Common Core State Standards for the target grade levels. Alignment charts are provided at the end of the book.

Each project focuses on a selected skill crucial to STEM learning; however, note that additional goals, big ideas, and essential questions are outlined in the introduction to each project:

- ▸ **Project 1:** Communicate effectively.
- ▸ **Project 2:** Focus on inquiry and collaboration.
- ▸ **Project 3:** Understand multiple content areas.
- ▸ **Project 4:** Explore contemporary issues.
- ▸ **Project 5:** Use technology, math, and reasoning.
- ▸ **Project 6:** Use and analyze models.
- ▸ **Project 7:** Record and analyze data.
- ▸ **Project 8:** Investigate change over time and patterns.
- ▸ **Project 9:** Use computer models or simulations.
- ▸ **Project 10:** Construct and explain systems.

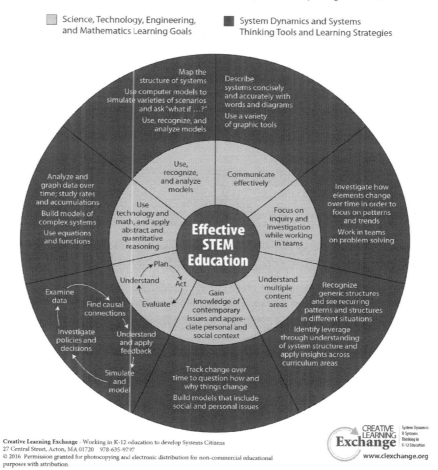

FIGURE 3. Effective STEM education. From "Using System Dynamics and Systems Thinking (SD/ST) Tools and Learning Strategies to Build Science, Technology, Engineering, and Math Excellence," by Creative Learning Exchange, 2016, retrieved from http://www.clexchange.org/curriculum/standards/stem.asp. Copyright 2016 by Creative Learning Exchange. Reprinted with permission.

① Communicate Effectively

The ability to communicate effectively—both verbally and in writing—is crucial to our students during their time in our classrooms and beyond. Consider a lawyer. He has to be able to write legal briefs that enable him to build his case. He also needs to communicate this brief to the judge or court in order to effectively represent his client. Doctors also use a combination of these skills. They have to be able to communicate effectively with their patients in order to explain what is going on, and they have to record what they learned into patients' files so that there is an established record of patients' health. These are simplified examples, but that does not diminish the importance of communication skills.

Teachers, especially, utilize communication in their profession, from teaching concepts to a class, to communicating with parents, administrators, and other stakeholders, and more. If a teacher is effectively going to provide feedback to students, he or she must be able to convey this feedback both in written and verbal form. This double reinforcement better equips students to learn from mistakes and strive for improvement in the future.

What does communication look like in a STEM project? It can take a variety of forms, depending on the product that students are asked to produce. For example, if students have been charged with defending a proposal for a design for a product they wish to market to an authentic panel, they will have to employ their speaking skills in order to effectively communicate their plan. Such a presentation requires a combination of style and substance—style in the manner in which the proposal is presented and substance in the quality of the information presented. Characteristics of high-quality presentations of this nature might include:

- The presentation can be clearly heard the entire time, and the participant speaks slowly and clearly throughout.
- The presenter's demeanor is professional throughout. It sounds as though the presentation has been rehearsed several times.
- The presentation is organized in a manner that makes it easy to follow and to understand what is going on at any given time.

If, however, students were charged with creating a brochure that conveyed the information for the project, they would have to communicate in written form. Characteristics of high-quality products of this nature might include:

- The brochure has little to no spelling/grammatical errors.
- The brochure is typed in a format that makes it easy to view.
- The brochure uses sentence structures that makes the paragraphs flow and easy to read.

No matter which style students are asked to communicate in, the substance needs to have the same quality. These descriptors could be used for either written or spoken products:

- The project is organized clearly, allowing someone to know what is being discussed at any given time.
- The student provides plenty of examples to back up statements made.
- The student provides much detail, explaining concepts and ideas so that someone can gain a full understanding of what is being talked about.

It is important that any project you present to students requires them to utilize both written and spoken skills so that students display competence in any venue. This will make them that much more effective when going out in the real world to find themselves a job. After all, the top job skills that companies are looking for in new hires all have to do with communication (Graduate Management Admission Council, 2014; see Figure 4). If you were to help your students master both written and verbal com-

1. Oral communication
2. Listening skills
3. Adaptability
4. Written communication
5. Presentation skills

6. Value opinions of others
7. Integrity
8. Follow a leader
9. Drive
10. Cross-cultural sensitivity

FIGURE 4. Top 10 skills sought by employers. Adapted from Graduate Management Admission Council, 2018.

munication, they would have an advantage over other potential hires who are less accomplished with these skills.

Create Your Own Crayon

In this project, students will design a new color. Then, they will develop and present a pitch about what makes their color original and why someone would want to use it. Students should present their pitches to a panel (e.g., other students, parents, administrators, etc.) as though they are pitching their color to Crayola and detailing why it should make a crayon featuring their color. Pitches should be no more than 2 minutes long. Once all students have presented, the panel members should select their top pitches.

Materials

▸ Read alouds about colors, such as *My Many Colored Days* by Dr. Seuss and *Mouse Paint* by Ellen Stohl Walsh
▸ Paper and finger paints (enough per student)
▸ Project Outline: Create Your Own Crayon (student copies)
▸ Suggested Timeline
▸ Lesson: What Are Primary Colors?
▸ Lesson: What Are Secondary Colors?
▸ Lesson: What Is a "Good" Color?
▸ Lesson: How to Develop a Pitch
▸ Handout 1.1: Peer Review (student copies)
▸ Product Rubric: Create Your Own Crayon (student copies)

PROJECT OUTLINE

Create Your Own Crayon

Big Idea

You can develop an original idea using existing ideas as a basis.

Essential Question

How does one express an idea to convince others of its value?

Deliverables

You will design a new color. Then, you will develop and present a pitch about what makes your color original and why someone would want to use it. You will address the audience as though you are pitching your color to Crayola and detailing why it should make a crayon featuring your color.

Constraints

Even though you will use familiar colors to create yours, your color has to be unique.

SUGGESTED TIMELINE

DAY				
1 Introduce the project and conduct Lesson: What Are Primary Colors? *Ask.*	**2** Conduct Lesson: What Are Secondary Colors? *Ask.*	**3** Conduct Lesson: What Is a "Good" Color? *Imagine.*	**4** Have students plan how they are going to create their colors. *Plan.*	**5** Have students experiment with creating their colors. *Create.*
6 Have students make a final version of their colors. *Create.*	**7** Conduct Lesson: How to Develop a Pitch. *Ask/ Imagine.*	**8** Have students work on their pitches. *Plan.*	**9** Have students practice their pitches with five different peers (see Handout 1.1). *Improve.*	**10** Have students present their pitches to a panel.

Project 1: Communicate Effectively

What Are Primary Colors?

1. Preassess students' knowledge about the primary colors. This can be written, be done in groups, or be a whole-class discussion.
   - How many primary colors are there? (Three.)
   - Name the primary colors. (Blue, red, and yellow.)
   - What makes them primary colors? (They cannot be mixed from other colors.)
   - Why are they important? (Possible answer: Because all other colors are made from these primary colors.)
   - What would happen if we did not have the primary colors? How might colors be different?

2. Ask students how they feel when they see these colors.
3. After getting some responses from students, read to the class the book *My Many Colored Days* by Dr. Seuss. After the story, talk about the different feelings the colors made the author feel and whether the students agree with these feelings or not.

What Are Secondary Colors?

1. Read aloud the book *Mouse Paint* by Ellen Stohl Walsh, in which three mice mix the primary colors to make new colors (or another book about secondary colors).
2. Introduce and/or review the secondary colors (orange, green, and purple) with students.
   - How do we get orange? (A combination of red and yellow.)
   - How do we get green? (A combination of blue and yellow.)
   - How do we get purple? (A combination of red and blue.)

3. Ask: What other colors could you make by combining colors? Examples might include:
   - Black and white = gray
   - Red and white = pink
   - Blue and orange = brown
   - Red and green = brown
   - Yellow and purple = brown
   - Colors can be lightened by adding white
   - Colors can be darkened by adding black

4. Ask: *Could you combine more than two colors? Could you take these combinations and combine them to make different colors?*

Project 1: Communicate Effectively

LESSON

What Is a "Good" Color?

1. Conduct a conversation about what makes an appealing color. Ask students:
   ▸ What is your favorite color?
   ▸ What does this color make you think of?
   ▸ Why do you think it is your favorite color?
   ▸ How would you convince someone else to like your favorite color?
   ▸ How do you think this color is created?
   ▸ Imagine a way that your favorite color could be even more appealing or pretty. What would that look like?

2. Supply students with a piece of white paper and some finger paint. You want them to have access to both primary and secondary colors. Let them experiment with many different colors, combining colors to create at least five different ones. Have them rank the colors they have created, choosing the one they feel is the prettiest, or what they consider to be a good color. Remind students that they will want to use the color they like the best to develop a pitch to Crayola as to why it should make a crayon featuring their color.

How to Develop a Pitch

1. Remind students that they will be developing a 2-minute pitch as to why Crayola should use their color in its new batch of colors.
2. Ask students: *What do you think a pitch is?*
3. Ask: *If you were trying to get someone to eat ice cream, how would you convince him or her to do this?* Possible answers might include:
   ▸ It is sweet.
   ▸ It is cold and refreshing.
   ▸ It combines flavors if you use toppings.
   ▸ It has a smooth texture.
   ▸ It has lots of possible flavors so you will probably find one you like.

4. Tell students: *This is a pitch. You are trying to convince someone to like something that you believe should be liked. You are going to be pitching your new color to a panel. You will have up to 2 minutes to present your pitch to the panel.*
5. Tell students that there are several things they should consider for their pitches, such as:
   ▸ how to introduce their color (e.g., its name, an image, a feeling it might cause),
   ▸ how enthusiastic they are about their new color (if they do not seem to care, why should anyone else?),
   ▸ specific reasons or examples why someone might like this color,
   ▸ speaking clearly so that the audience can understand them and that they are loud enough for people to hear them, and
   ▸ having a strong finish, making sure to give anyone listening something to think about.

Project 1: Communicate Effectively

Name: _____ Date: _____

HANDOUT 1.1

Peer Review

Directions: With a partner, listen to each other's pitches. Listen and look for qualities of good presentation skills.

1. Is your partner clear in his or her explanation?

2. Is he or she easy to understand?

3. Is he or she loud enough?

4. Does he or she make occasional eye contact with the audience, or is she always looking down or elsewhere?

5. Does he or she stand up straight and keep his or her hands out of his or her pockets?

6. Does he or she speak for longer than a minute?

If you do not hear or see a lot of these things, suggest ways your partner can improve his or her pitch. For example, if you thought your partner was not easy to understand, what could he or she do differently to be better understood?

Listen to your partner's feedback about your pitch.

Then, practice your pitch with four other students, repeating the steps above.

After you have practiced your pitch with five classmates, reflect on what you have learned to make your pitch better based on your classmates' suggestions. Revise your pitch as needed.

PRODUCT RUBRIC

Create Your Own Crayon

	The Pitch	The Evidence
Great	Student is very clear in his or her explanation in both content and voice, making a specific argument as to why his or her color should be picked by the panel.	Student provides many examples of how his or her color can be used and why people might like it.
Good	Student makes an argument for his or her color, but it is not always organized or clear, or it may be hard to hear.	Student provides a couple of examples of how his or her color can be used and why people might like it, but some more evidence would have made a stronger point.
Needs Improvement	Student does not make an argument, or the argument he or she provides makes no sense.	Student does not provide any examples of how someone might use his or her color, making it hard to know why someone might like it.

Project 1: Communicate Effectively

2 Focus on Inquiry and Collaboration

Students should be engaging in inquiry on a daily basis. Through inquiry, students discover things for themselves, much like they did when they were young children first learning about their place in the world. Inquiry is what caused them to first discover what got their parents' attention or first emulate another person's actions. Oftentimes the inquiry came from experimenting with something and, if it did not work, learning from mistakes.

The best way to facilitate an environment of inquiry in the classroom is through teaching students to ask the right sorts of questions. Younger students, especially, may need more guidance as to what form these questions will take. And the subject matter students are inquiring about should be rather subjective. If you get into a discussion about what color the sky is, the answer is always going to come down to blue. If, however, you have a more open-ended inquiry, such as what brand of pizza is best or whether it is ever okay to lie, the conversation is going to be endless because there is no correct answer.

Fostering inquiry is what the engineering design process (see Figure 2) is all about. In each and every step, students discover new ideas and concepts for themselves. When they start, they are discovering the problems and constraints by asking questions. They then come up with ideas and a plan, letting their imaginations run wild. The next step involves experimenting with materials and what it will take to make students' ideas come alive. Finally, students look at what they have done and try to make it better, inquiring as to what this might look like.

Part of this process is also having the ability to fail. Failure used to have such a negative connotation in education. Failing a class meant you were not doing well. Now there is a new outlook on failure. Fail actually stands for "first attempt in learning." There should be a space in the classroom where students can make mistakes without fear. This should especially be present during the improve phase of the engineering design process, where students must weigh what has worked, what has not, and figure out how to make the product better. The only way they are going to be able to do this successfully is if they can mess up in the first place.

The ability to work in a group and collaborate is a valuable 21st-century skill that is important to teach, even to young children. Students need to know how to resolve differences with classmates, divvy up tasks amongst peers, and produce something together they would have been unable to produce by themselves. Teachers cannot just put them into groups and hope for the best.

One way to ensure that students are working well together is to give each an individual role that will help the group. This way, instead of five people all trying to take charge, each student has a specific area to specialize in, which will make the quality of the product that much better. If each group member focuses on his or her job, the product the group creates should be better than if any member had worked on it on his or her own. There will likely need to be some conversation about the roles. For example, just making a student the leader might not be enough for him or her to succeed in that role. There might need to be a discussion about what a good leader does. Other roles should also be clearly laid out. If there is room for interpretation, it is best to have a discussion as a class as to what the role should look like.

Once students have been given these roles, there is clear accountability. If something was not written down, it is the scribe who is responsible for it. If a direction was left out of the final product, the quality controller should have caught it. This accountability takes out that mob mentality where everyone in the group is held equally accountable. Even though students are given specific tasks, however, it is important for them to see how collaborating enabled them to develop a better product together.

Art Bot

In this project, using just a handful of supplies, students will work in groups to build mechanized Art Bots that will contribute to a class piece of art. When students complete the construction of their Art Bots, bring all of the Art Bots together on a very large piece of paper on the floor to host an Art Bot Rally. Then, have students reflect upon the piece their collective robots created. They can do this in written form, in a discussion, in a small-group setting, or through a combination:

- **Describe:** What do you see?
- **Analyze:** How does the piece of art make you feel?
- **Interpret:** What do you think the artist was trying to say with the art?
- **Evaluate:** Do you like this piece of art?

Note. Handout 2.2 (see Materials list) details how to construct an Art Bot. See https://blueprint.digitalharbor.org/sample-projects/art-bots for photos and helpful tips (if needed). There are also videos of Art Bots in action available on YouTube if you or your students need to visualize this project.

Materials

- Art Bot supplies for each group of five students: scissors, 5 rubber bands, one inexpensive electric toothbrush (batteries if needed), 3–4 markers, one paper cup (acquire a variety of paper cups so groups can decide which size/style to use), decorations (e.g., pipe cleaners, craft sticks, googly eyes, masking tape), blank sheets of paper
- Large piece of butcher paper (for large class piece of art)
- Project Outline: Art Bot (student copies)
- Suggested Timeline
- Lesson: What Is "Good" Art?
- Lesson: How to Analyze Art
- Handout 2.1: Analyzing Art (student copies)
- Handout 2.2: Building Your Art Bot (student copies)

PROJECT OUTLINE

Art Bot

Big Idea

Science, technology, engineering, art, and math (STEAM) can work together.

Essential Question

How can we use engineering and technology to make art?

Deliverables

You will work with a group in order to create an Art Bot that will contribute to a class piece of art.

Constraints

You may only use the following supplies:
▸ a few rubber bands,
▸ one inexpensive electric toothbrush,
▸ three or four markers, and
▸ a paper cup.

SUGGESTED TIMELINE

DAY				
1 Introduce the project and conduct Lesson: What Is "Good" Art? *Ask.*	**2** Conduct Lesson: How to Analyze Art. *Imagine.*	**3** Have students work in groups to create Art Bots. *Plan/Create.*	**4** Have students test their Art Bots. *Improve.*	**5** Host an Art Bot Rally. Have students complete a reflection.

What Is "Good" Art?

1. Display for students a variety of paintings (many are available online), such as:
   - *Mona Lisa* by Leonardo da Vinci
   - *Still Life With Compote and Glass* by Pablo Picasso
   - *The Scream* by Edvard Munch
   - *The Persistence of Memory* by Salvador Dali
   - *Campbell's Soup Cans* by Andy Warhol
   - *Convergence* by Jackson Pollock

2. Ask students to discuss whether they think these paintings are good or not. Have them share their thoughts and feelings. Students may discuss as a class or in small groups. Some questions students might want to ponder for each painting include:
   - Do you like the painting?
   - What do you like or not like about it?
   - What could be changed for you to like it more?
   - Can you see how others might or might not like the painting?
   - Would you consider it art? Why or why not?

How to Analyze Art

1. Tell students that there are four steps to analyzing art: describe, analyze, interpret, and evaluate. Students may consider these steps by analyzing a pumpkin like a piece of art.

2. Describe: *How would you describe a regular pumpkin?* Have students describe a typical pumpkin. They might point out things such as its orange color, the waxiness of its surface, the stem at the top, or the ribs that divide the pumpkin up into sections. Most of the responses may be surface level because that is what students see with their eyes. Tell students: *When you first begin to look at art, this is usually where we start. We ask questions such as* (Center for Writers, n.d.):

   ▶ What is the first thing that catches your eye in this piece?
   ▶ What else did you notice?
   ▶ Is there anything you see in the artwork?
   ▶ List all of the objects and shapes that you can see.
   ▶ What do you think is happening in this work of art?
   ▶ Does anything you have noticed remind you of something in your own life?
   ▶ What makes this artwork look realistic or unrealistic to you?
   ▶ Is the subject of the artwork a color, a shape, or a feeling? Or does the artwork tell a specific story?

3. Analyze: *What would you say if I asked you to explain what is inside of a pumpkin?* Students may share their past experiences, or you might want to bring a pumpkin in, depending on the season, and open it up. Students should explain how inside the pumpkin are its guts. Prod them to explain what these guts look like. What else makes up the inside of a pumpkin, and what is each of these parts used for? Tell students that analyzing art means to look "at the way the artist used the elements of design (color, line, shape, form, texture, space) and the principles of design (rhythm, balance, contrast, movement, center of interest, repetition, variety)" (Center for Writers, n.d., para. 3). Say: *By analyzing, you are basically trying to go inside the painting. We ask questions such as:*

   ▶ How did the artist use shapes, lines, and form to construct this artwork? What effect do these have?
   ▶ What is at the center of the artwork? What attracts you to this?
   ▶ Is there anything that really draws your attention to the artwork? What is it? What about the art draws you to it? Are there things that seem less important? How are they portrayed?

Lesson: How to Analyze Art, *continued*

4. Interpret: *What can turn a pumpkin into art?* Students could talk about how you could carve it into a jack-o'-lantern, or how it can be decorated with colors, or how it might be turned into a delicious pumpkin pie. Tell students: *Interpretation is "discovering the meaning or the story behind a work of art"* (Center for Writers, n.d., para. 4). *We ask questions such as:*
    ▶ What does this artwork make you feel? What objects, lines, colors, or shapes cause you to feel this way?
    ▶ What story do you think this piece of art is telling? How is it told?
    ▶ How do you think the artist might have felt when he or she made this work of art? What clues are there to this?

5. Evaluate: *What makes a pumpkin good?* Students may mention how delicious a pumpkin pie is, the size of the pumpkin, or the detail of a pumpkin carving. Tell students: *Evaluation requires "forming your own opinions and explaining why you have them"* (Center for Writers, n.d., para. 5). *We ask questions such as:*
    ▶ Do you think this is a good piece of art? What about it makes you feel this way?
    ▶ What do you think your reactions to this piece of art say about you as a person?
    ▶ Do you think the artist has clearly told the story or expressed the emotion he or she wanted to portray in the artwork?

6. Have student analyze a piece of art using these guidelines (see Handout 2.1). Have a discussion about their answers for each of the descriptors.

HANDOUT 2.1

Analyzing Art

Directions: As you analyze a work of art, answer the following questions. Use as much detail as possible.

1. **Describe:** What do you see?

2. **Analyze:** How does the piece of art make you feel?

3. **Interpret:** What do you think the artist was trying to say with the art?

4. **Evaluate:** Do you like this piece of art?

Project 2: Focus on Inquiry and Collaboration

HANDOUT 2.2

Building Your Art Bot

Directions: You will be working in a group of five to develop your Art Bot. Each group member should have a specific role:

- **Picker:** This person is responsible for the decisions the group makes, making sure that there is a majority of people who want what is chosen.
- **Carver:** This person is responsible for the details, making sure that everything is where it needs to be.
- **Farmer:** This person is the leader of the group, making sure that goals and objectives are being followed and things are moving forward.
- **County fair judge:** This person determines if what the group has done is of quality work.
- **Harvester:** This person is the timekeeper, making sure that the group is not spending too much time on any one thing and finishes on time.

Time

- One class period

Materials

- Scissors
- 5 rubber bands
- 1 inexpensive electric toothbrush (batteries as needed)
- 3–4 markers
- 1 paper cup
- Decorations (pipe cleaners, craft sticks, googly eyes, masking tape— be creative!)
- Blank paper (for testing your Art Bot)

Name: _____ Date: _____

Assembly

1. Put a battery in your toothbrush and turn it on. This is your Art Bot's motor. Make sure it works!

2. Discuss amongst your group and choose how you will attach your robot motor to the paper cup. The paper cup acts as a simple body (or "housing") for your toothbrush. This housing will help your Art Bot move around.

3. Decorate your cup. Using googly eyes, pipe cleaners, and/or other materials, give your Art Bot some personality.

4. Cut a hole in the bottom of the paper cup large enough for the toothbrush to fit through. Insert your toothbrush into the center of the paper cup in a way that allows the vibration to move the cup. (*Note.* Depending on the size of your cup, you may need to remove the bristled head of the toothbrush so that it fits.)

5. Using the rubber bands, attach a few of the markers to the outside of the paper cup. These will act as your Art Bot's legs!

6. Align the markers so your Art Bot moves smoothly. Remove the caps on the markers. Set your Art Bot on a blank piece of paper. Check that the tips of your markers are the only things touching the paper. Check that the markers are touching the paper evenly. This will ensure that when your Art Bot starts drawing, all of the markers will be able to draw.

7. Make sure your Art Bot is set down on a sheet of paper. Turn on the motor, and watch your Art Bot go to work making beautiful art. Look at the patterns it is making. Be ready to catch your Art Bot if it tries to leave the paper!

Note. This activity is adapted from Digital Harbor Foundation, 2018.

3 Understand Multiple Content Areas

Once in the real world, students have to be able to pull different skills learned in separate arenas and put them together. Different subjects and skills work together to get desired results. What if schools facilitated more opportunities for students to build crosscurricular skills? STEM education is a perfect example of combining subject areas. Many educators include art in STEM education, known as STEAM. Others, still, include reading (STREAM), as there are connections to English language arts and literacy across the curriculum, such as writing a research paper, reading for comprehension, or conducting an interview. The sooner you expose students to a crosscurricular model, the better, as crosscurricular learning results in more authentic learning. Through crosscurricular lessons and activities, students can better understand the context of what they are learning and how it fits into the real world.

You know crosscurricular learning is working when students are utilizing skills from various subject areas—perhaps without even realizing the connections at first. If students are writing a research paper on the importance of various modes of transportation, such as the railroad, steamboats, and national roads, they may not realize they are learning about history while doing so or, alternatively, might not realize they are using language arts skills to learn about history. Or, during a science project involving the creation of a new version of a mousetrap, students may not realize the math skills they are developing by drawing a plan with dimensions.

The advantages to this integrated learning for students are many. A comprehensive study on "The Logic of Interdisciplinary Studies" (Mathison & Feeman, 1997) discovered that students experienced:

▸ an increase in understanding, retention, and application of general concepts;

▸ a better overall comprehension of global interdependencies, along with the development of multiple perspectives, points of view, and values;

▸ an increase in the ability to make decisions, think critically and creatively, and synthesize knowledge beyond the disciplines;

▸ the increased ability to identify, assess and transfer significant information needed for solving novel problems;

▸ the promotion of cooperative learning, a better attitude toward the self as a learner and as a meaningful member of a community; and

▸ increased motivation (pp. 19–20).

Integrated approaches make learning more organic and less forced. As human beings we are natural learners. From the moment we are born, we are learning every single second through experience. And yet, in school, we often take these experiences away and try to make what is being taught rigid and artificial. By using integrated learning, we allow students to experience how these subject areas all work together in the natural order of things. When learning is more natural, so are the results.

Bubblegum

In this project, students will work in groups to create a 30-second commercial that convinces others to buy a brand of gum. Students can use a tablet or smartphone to record their commercials. In the commercials, they must convey:

▸ why someone should chew this gum (students can use information from their science experiment),

- ▸ how to chew gum responsibly (students may use reasons from their debate on chewing gum in school), and
- ▸ a slogan (students can use aspects of their poems).

Students should plan the commercials first, making decisions as a group. Then they will have 2 days to shoot the commercial. These commercials can then be uploaded to YouTube or another video sharing site and shared with the class.

Materials

- ▸ A jar full of gumballs of various colors
- ▸ Three different brands of gum (enough for the class experiment)
- ▸ Project Outline: Bubblegum (student copies)
- ▸ Suggested Timeline
- ▸ Lesson: How Many Gumballs Are in the Jar?
- ▸ Lesson: The Social Responsibility of Chewing Gum
- ▸ Lesson: Which Gum Lasts the Longest?
- ▸ Lesson: Expressing Gum Through Poetry
- ▸ Handout 3.1: Rating Gum Flavors (student copies)
- ▸ Handout 3.2: Troublesome Bubble
- ▸ Product Rubric: Bubblegum (student copies)

PROJECT OUTLINE

Bubblegum

Big Idea

The same topic can be explored through math, science, language arts, and social studies.

Essential Question

How does one convince others to want something?

Deliverables

You will work with a group to create a 30-second commercial that convinces others to buy a brand of gum while not contributing to the gum pollution.

Constraints

The commercial
▸ must be 30 seconds long,
▸ must have a slogan, and
▸ must inform viewers about how to use gum responsibly.

SUGGESTED TIMELINE

DAY				
1 Introduce the project and conduct Lesson: How Many Gumballs Are in the Jar? *Ask*.	**2** Conduct Lesson: The Social Responsibility of Chewing Gum. *Ask*.	**3** Conduct Lesson: Which Gum Lasts the Longest? *Ask*.	**4** Conduct Lesson: Expressing Gum Through Poetry. *Ask/ Imagine*.	**5** Have students share their haikus.
6 Have students plan their commercials. *Ask/Plan*.	**7** Have students plan their commercials. *Plan*.	**8** Have students create their commercials. *Create*.	**9** Have students create their commercials. *Create/Improve*.	**10** Have students present their commercials.

Project 3: Understand Multiple Content Areas

LESSON

How Many Gumballs Are in the Jar?

1. Display for students a jar full of gumballs of various colors. Have students make several predictions about the jar of gumballs, such as:
   - Guess the number of bubble gum balls in the machine.
   - Guess which color you think there is the most of in the jar.

2. Then, have students determine the actual number and quantity of each color gumball. Record the number of each color on a class bar graph to represent the data.

3. Ask students to reflect:
   - How did you come up with your guess?
   - How close was your guess to the actual number?
   - If your guess was way off, what would you change in future predictions?
   - If your guess was close, do you think the strategy you used was the reason for this?
   - How can we make guesses a little closer?

Project 3: Understand Multiple Content Areas

LESSON

The Social Responsibility Of Chewing Gum

Positive Aspects of Gum	Negative Aspects of Gum
It tastes good.	It is messy.
It's fun to blow bubbles.	Bubbles can be distracting.
It calms people.	Loud chewing is annoying.
It keeps your mouth from being dry.	Dried gum is difficult to clean up.
It can help with a craving.	There might not be enough to share.

FIGURE 5. Positive versus negative aspects of gum.

1. Draw a two-column chart on the board. Label one side as the positive aspects of gum, and label the other side as the negative aspects of gum.
2. Have students either generate ideas verbally as you write, or have students write responses on sticky notes and place them on the chart. Some possible responses for students to think about are included in Figure 5.
3. Divide students into pairs for a debate. Have students flip a coin or roll dice to determine who should debate in favor of which position:
   ▸ Gum should be allowed in school.
   ▸ Gum should not be allowed in school.

4. Have students debate against their partners, making the arguments for their position.
5. To present their side of the debate, students should state their position, discuss three examples to support their position, and then restate their position. For example, "I think kids should be allowed to chew gum in school. This will teach kids to be responsible because they will need to throw it away once they are done. This will encourage kids to share because gum usually comes in a pack. It also helps them to relax. And that's why I think kids should be allowed to chew gum in school."

LESSON

Which Gum Lasts the Longest?

1. Tell students: *Scientists conduct all sorts of different experiments, but they usually all involve the scientific method. The scientific method is just the order of steps you go through to make sure your experiment is effective.*

2. Tell students that they will conduct an experiment concerning which gum brand lasts the longest. As a class, students will go through the first six steps together:

   ▸ State the problem in the form of a question: Which gum brand lasts the longest?

   ▸ State your hypothesis: A hypothesis is just your educated guess. Students can make their own hypotheses for which of the three brands of gum they believe will last the longest, or you can put it to a class vote. Students should also have in mind why they picked the brand they did.

   ▸ Make a list of the materials necessary to carry out the experiment: Students will need three different brands of gum, one record sheet per student or team (see Handout 3.1), and pencils or other writing utensils.

   ▸ List the procedures in chronological order: There will be three rounds of chewing, each lasting 5 minutes and timed by the teacher. Students will chew one piece of gum, rating it every minute on a scale of very strong to no flavor at all. Students will record these ratings on Handout 3.1. Repeat these steps for a total of three different brands of gum.

   ▸ Indicate the variables: Provide a basic definition. A variable is something that could affect the outcome of the experiment. Are all three brands the same flavor, or is one spearmint, while another is cinnamon? The ratings are based on personal opinion. What if different people rate the brands differently based on their tastes? Is the order students taste the gums in having an effect because the flavor from the past gum might still be in their mouths?

   ▸ Create charts and graphs to record your observed results: Students will record their findings on their data sheets (see Handout 3.1).

   ▸ State your conclusion: Students will then determine which gum they actually thought lasted the longest and compare this to their hypothesis. Alternatively, you could tabulate the opinions of the class, saying a majority thought one brand lasted the longest and using that to determine the experiment.

Expressing Gum Through Poetry

1. Have students read the poem "Troublesome Bubble" (see Handout 3.2). Afterward, discuss:
   ▸ How does the poem make you feel?
   ▸ What is the tone of the poem?
   ▸ How was its use of rhyme?

2. Then, have each student write a haiku about how it feels to chew gum. Students should include one or more of the five senses in the poem: feel, hear, taste, touch, and smell. Tell students that a haiku is a three-line poem that does not rhyme. The first line is five syllables, the second line is seven syllables, and the third line is five syllables. A haiku often features an image meant to show the feeling of a specific moment in time.

HANDOUT 3.1

Rating Gum Flavors

Directions: Keep track of your observations on this sheet. Include as much detail as possible.

1. State the problem in the form of a question.

2. State your hypothesis.

3. Make a list of the materials necessary to carry out the experiment.

4. Write down the procedures.

5. Indicate the variables.

Handout 3.1: Rating Gum Flavors, *continued*

6. Create charts and graphs to record your observed results. Use additional sheets of paper as needed.

7. State your conclusion.

How Long Does the Flavor Last?

Brand 1: _____

Flavor: _____

Flavor Strength Recording Chart			
	Very Strong	**Somewhat Strong**	**Taste Still Present**	**Weak**
After 1 minute				
After 2 minutes				
After 3 minutes				
After 4 minutes				
After 5 minutes				

Project 3: Understand Multiple Content Areas

Name: _____ Date: _____

Handout 3.1: Rating Gum Flavors, *continued*

Brand 2: _____

Flavor: _____

Flavor Strength Recording Chart				
	Very Strong	**Somewhat Strong**	**Taste Still Present**	**Weak**
After 1 minute				
After 2 minutes				
After 3 minutes				
After 4 minutes				
After 5 minutes				

10 Performance-Based STEM Projects for Grades K–1 © Prufrock Press Inc.

Name: _____ Date: _____

Handout 3.1: Rating Gum Flavors, *continued*

Brand 3: _____

Flavor: _____

Flavor Strength Recording Chart				
	Very Strong	**Somewhat Strong**	**Taste Still Present**	**Weak**
After 1 minute				
After 2 minutes				
After 3 minutes				
After 4 minutes				
After 5 minutes				

Project 3: Understand Multiple Content Areas

HANDOUT 3.2

Troublesome Bubble

I was sitting in class one cold, dreary day
Daydreaming my boring class time away
When I reached into my pocket and found
A tiny object that was tied and bound

I slipped it out and immediately saw
It was something expressly meant for my jaw
A piece of gum I'd forgotten about
So I unwrapped it and quickly took it out

I had to be careful—I couldn't get caught
Gum in the classroom was something not
Allowed by our teacher—she had been quite clear
Being found with gum in your mouth was something to fear

Why, a boy had been trapped just last week
And since that time we haven't heard a peep
Where he's gone to we don't really have a hunch
But the rumor is he's been turned to lunch

To chew the gum risked life and limb
But I loved gum even more than gym
The sugary smell was too much to take
This was a dangerous mission I had to make

I slipped the small piece between my lips
And on the sugar coating I began to sip
As the sweet, sweet taste covered my tongue
I quietly tried to chew my gum

Handout 3.2: Troublesome Bubble, *continued*

But the taste was so good—I got carried away
And began to chew like a cow with her hay
I expected to get caught—I was ready to sing
But the teacher was too busy doing her thing

This lack of detection gave me a sense
Of confidence, added to a flavor quite intense
I began to chew harder—I just had to deplete
All of the tang out of this one little piece

It happened quite quickly—it ran out of taste
So now all my chewing was going to waste
There was one last thing to do with my confection
If my teacher would simply look in the other direction

Although I tried to fight, I couldn't resist
There was no denying I just had to do it
I couldn't ignore—it was like an addiction
As for you, the reader, you can make the prediction

I put my tongue in the gum and began to push
On the soft wad of blubber I had chewed to a mush
It grew bigger and bigger and before I could stop
It got out of control and gave quite a loud pop

My teacher halted her lesson and came to my desk
It would probably've been better if I had simply confessed
When she asked me what all the noise was about
I turned to my teacher and left it no doubt

All over my nose was a rubbery mess
As my teacher scowled at me over the desk
There was no denying the gum on my face
That troublesome bubble had just sealed my fate

PRODUCT RUBRIC

Bubblegum

	The Commercial	Content
Great	The slogan is catchy and easy to repeat. The commercial can be seen and heard easily.	The commercial provides a clear explanation as to why someone should chew the gum. It gives a clear example of how to chew gum responsibly.
Good	The slogan is somewhat catchy but not easy to repeat. The commercial can be seen or heard easily, but not both.	The commercial provides an explanation as to why someone should chew this gum, but it is not fully convincing. It gives an example of how to chew gum responsibly, but it is not completely clear.
Needs Improvement	The slogan is either not present or is not catchy. The commercial cannot be seen and heard easily.	The commercial does not provide an explanation as to why someone should chew this gum. It does not give an example of how to chew gum responsibly.

4 Explore Contemporary Issues

Students learn reading, writing, and arithmetic, but we also hope that they will learn to be better people during their time in school. This starts by having awareness—first of those immediately around them. We can grow students' awareness by teaching them to be polite and considerate of their classmates, teachers, and other school community staff through character education. Then, this immediate environment can be expanded to include the community that they live in. What are the town's problems? What can students do to help or contribute more to their community? This grows and grows, expanding to their country and then, ideally, to global awareness.

Global awareness means more than being aware of current events going on around the world. According to the Partnership for 21st Century Skills (2016), global awareness entails:

- Using 21st century skills to understand and address global issues
- Learning from and working collaboratively with individuals representing diverse cultures, religions and lifestyles in a spirit of mutual respect and open dialogue in personal, work and community contexts
- Understanding other nations and cultures, including the use of non-English languages (p. 2)

Global awareness helps students to understand and appreciate personal and social context. Personal context refers to the intrapersonal environment that shapes an individual's experience. Such environmental factors play a role in determining the student's response to experiences and interactions. If a person is prejudiced against someone else or another group or culture, it is probably due to an experience or something that was relayed to him or her that caused such a response. People do not choose to be prejudiced; rather their intrapersonal environment often shapes them into being that way. Social context is recognizing that sometimes your own personal context and that of those around you are not necessarily the same. As an example, this has come up in the news recently: Personal tweets authored by public figures many years ago when they were younger and less aware of the social context of their comments are coming to light, and these individuals are now facing the repercussions. The lesson here is that your digital footprint is there forever. A comment you once made might have been fine in the personal context of your friends, but once exposed to the public, it can come back to haunt you.

To help students become more aware, expose them to contemporary issues that society is dealing with. This could be something that is happening in your town, a cause that needs support, or a worldwide problem, such as hunger or lack of an education. Showing students that they can make a difference can have an effect on their personal context. They might see something from another point of view or gain an understanding of something they were previously ignorant about.

Community service projects are an excellent way for students to learn about contemporary issues, as well as use the engineering design process to problem solve. Whether gathering canned foods for the local pantry, educating others about the opioid epidemic, raising money for kids with cancer, or trying to create practical solutions for farming in third-world countries, students will gain an awareness of the people in these situations and develop empathy. One thing that can frustrate students, especially younger ones, is feeling like there is nothing they can do about a problem. They hear about children starving in Africa, hurricanes that devastate Puerto Rico, or the homeless people in their town, and empathize with the people who are affected. Helping students to understand how they can help not only makes them aware of the problem, but it also makes them aware of what can be done about it.

Recycling, Huh! What Is It Good For?

In this project, students will make an object out of only recycled materials. Their objects must be things that can be used for a practical purpose (e.g., a piggy bank made out of an oatmeal container, a bird feeder made out of a soda bottle, a game made out of cardboard, a flower pot made out of a glass container, etc.). Students will display their objects in a final exhibition in which each student's object must have a sign in front of it detailing what the object is and which recycled materials it is made from.

Materials

- ▸ A variety of recyclable materials (for student projects)
- ▸ Student computer and Internet access
- ▸ Project Outline: Recycling, Huh! What Is It Good For? (student copies)
- ▸ Suggested Timeline
- ▸ Lesson: What Is Recycling?
- ▸ Lesson: What Is Recyclable?
- ▸ Lesson: What Are the Benefits of Recycling?
- ▸ Product Rubric: Recycling, Huh! What Is It Good For? (student copies)

PROJECT OUTLINE

Recycling, Huh! What Is It Good For?

Big Idea

Recycling can help the planet.

Essential Question

How can we recycle materials for a practical purpose?

Deliverables

You are going to make an object out of only recycled materials. This object must be something that can be used for a practical purpose, which means it can be used for an everyday task. You will then display your objects in a final exhibition. During the final exhibition, your object must have a sign in front of it detailing what the object is and which recycled materials it is made from.

Constraints

Your object:

▸ must be made out of recyclable objects and materials, and

▸ must have a practical purpose.

SUGGESTED TIMELINE

DAY				
1 Introduce the project and conduct Lesson: What Is Recycling? *Ask*.	**2** Conduct Lesson: What Is Recyclable? *Ask*.	**3** Conduct Lesson: What Are the Benefits of Recycling? *Ask*.	**4** Have students begin to plan their objects, making a list of recyclable materials they need to construct them. *Imagine*.	**5** Have students continue to plan their objects. *Plan*.
6 Have students bring in materials and begin to build their objects. *Create*.	**7** Have students continue to build their objects. *Create*.	**8** Have students continue to build their objects. *Create*.	**9** Have students improve their objects. *Improve*.	**10** Host a final exhibition in which students display their objects.

LESSON

What Is Recycling?

1. Ask students: *Can anyone tell me what recycling means?* (It means to reuse materials rather than putting them in the trash. We try to find objects or parts of objects that can used again, and find a new purpose for them.)

2. Show a YouTube video that shows what recycling is, such as "How Recycling Works!" by SciShow Kids (available at https://www.youtube.com/watch?v=VlRVPum9cp4).

3. Ask students:

   ▸ *When* do you recycle? (Whenever possible, but only certain things can be recycled. You have to make sure the items you are earmarking for recycling can actually be recycled.)

   ▸ *Where* does one recycle? (You can recycle almost anywhere. Most trash companies have a service where they will pick up your recyclables separately from your regular trash. Schools run recycling programs where there is a recycling wastepaper basket in each room and then students collect the recyclables. There are drop-off sites where people can go to turn over their recyclables.)

   ▸ *Who* can recycle? (The good news is that almost anyone can recycle. You do have to be organized when you recycle, however, as well as diligent. Keeping the recyclables separate from the regular trash can be a challenging job. And finding places to send your recyclables can sometimes be difficult.)

   ▸ *How* does recycling work? Show a video on how paper is recycled (e.g., "The Paper Recycling Process" by Domtar, available at https://www.youtube.com/watch?v=jAqVxsEgWIM) and/or how plastic bottles are recycled (e.g., "Life of a Plastic Bottle" by PepsiCo Recycling, available at https://www.youtube.com/watch?v=erGnf7ws20E).

   ▸ *Why* should we recycle? (The planet only has so many resources. If we keep using new resources all of the time, eventually we are going to run out.)

What Is Recyclable?

1. Ask students to generate a list of recyclables. You can use the following categories if students get stuck:
    ▸   Paper: Books, newspapers, magazines, cardboard boxes (e.g., corrugated cardboard, cereal boxes, tissue boxes), envelopes, phone books, paper towel/toilet paper rolls, junk mail, etc.
    ▸   Plastic: Water bottles, plastic wrappers, plastic containers, etc.
    ▸   Glass: Bottles, jars, old light bulbs, plates, drinking glasses, etc.
    ▸   Metal: Aluminum soda cans, tin cans, whipped cream or aerosol canisters, metal hangers, small appliances (e.g., toasters, irons, coffee makers, kitchen mixers, pots and pans), etc.

2. Consider creating a two-column class chart. In one column, you can list things you can recycle, and in the other you can list things you cannot. You can list items on sticky notes, and then have students go up to the chart and place them on the correct side. The class can correct any mistakes or have discussions about things that may be recyclable if cleaned but cannot be recycled if dirty.

3. Explain that almost as important as what you recycle is what you often cannot recycle, such as:
    ▸   loose plastic bags;
    ▸   plastic shopping bags;
    ▸   plastic stretch wrap;
    ▸   polystyrene foam cups, egg cartons, or containers;
    ▸   dirty take-out containers;
    ▸   dirty drinking cups;
    ▸   soiled food containers and paper products (e.g., pizza boxes and fast food containers that have grease, which makes items difficult to recycle); and
    ▸   broken or sharp glass.

4. (Optional) Have students research their own city/town's recycling rules/procedures so that the discussion is specific to them.

What Are the Benefits of Recycling?

1. In order to reinforce the lesson on what is and what is not recyclable, have students take part in an interactive activity by playing the recycling game available at https://www.learningliftoff.com/teaching-kids-recycling.
2. Share with students a video on the benefits of recycling, such as "The Impact of the Recycling Industry," available at https://www.youtube.com/watch?v=-ou9dvTpz7k.
3. Then, individually, in groups, or as a class, have students generate a list of the benefits of recycling. They might consider:
   ▸ Recycling reduces humans' environmental footprint.
   ▸ If you did not recycle, you might eventually run out of materials.
   ▸ Recycling saves energy because it takes more energy to produce items with raw materials than from recycling. It is also more expensive to create objects using new materials.
   ▸ Recycling keeps air pollution down because materials that are not recycled are sometimes incinerated in a trash-burning power plant, polluting the air.
   ▸ Recycling reduces the size of landfills. A lot of unrecycled garbage gets put into landfills.
   ▸ Recycling provides employment opportunities. Just throwing trash away employs 6–7 people, while recycling creates close to 30 jobs.
   ▸ You can be rewarded for your recycling efforts because aluminum cans, glass bottles, and old newspapers can sometimes be sold to places for profit.
   ▸ Recycling brings people together through recycling drives and a common cause.
   ▸ Recycling protects ecosystems and wildlife. Instead of having to cut down new trees for paper products and taking away an organism's habitat, you can avoid this by reusing materials.
   ▸ Recycling helps people who might have been relocated because of the resources near them that needed to be taken.

Name: _____ Date: _____

PRODUCT RUBRIC

Recycling, Huh! What Is It Good For?

	Object	Display
Great	The object is made of completely recyclable materials. The object serves a practical purpose; someone could use it.	The object is well put together, making its purpose clear. There is a sign in front of the object saying which recycled materials were used.
Good	Most of the object is made of recyclable materials but not all. The object serves a practical purpose, but it may not be able to be used by someone.	The object's purpose is clear, but it could be put together better. There is a sign in front of the object listing its name but not which recycled materials were used.
Needs Improvement	The object is mostly made of nonrecyclable materials. The object does not serve a practical purpose.	The object is not put together well, making it difficult to see its purpose. There is no sign in front of the object.

Project 4: Explore Contemporary Issues

5 Use Technology, Math, and Reasoning

Abstract reasoning can be a challenge for students, especially younger ones. This is because they think very much in concrete terms; this or that, black or white, wrong or right. What does it mean to be an abstract thinker? An abstract thinker:

- ▸ can understand and separate context from content;
- ▸ is able to understand relationships between events or can connect the dots;
- ▸ understands the meaning behind words, situations, and events;
- ▸ draws generalizations from a specific set of circumstances; and
- ▸ has the ability to compare different situations.

According to Stanley (2018), you might hear an abstract thinker "say, 'I wonder . . .' or 'What if this happened . . . ?' They are able to think about situations that are not there, but other students may only be able to think about what is right in front of them" (p. 173). In the classroom, abstract thinkers:

- ▸ are able to use metaphors and analogies with ease;
- ▸ can understand the relationship between both verbal and nonverbal ideas;

- possess complex reasoning skills, such as critical thinking and problem solving;
- can mentally maneuver objects without having to physically do it, known as spatial reasoning;
- are adept at imagining situations that have happened or are not actually happening; and
- appreciate sarcasm. (p. 173)

Math has a lot of abstract thinking. Even the act of learning to count has many abstract qualities to it, such as (Scholastic, n.d.):

- **The stable-order rule:** Saying counting words only once and in a consistent order (e.g., "seven, eight, nine . . .").
- **The cardinal rule:** Giving a summary or "how many" total. When starting out, children might have to recount to remember the total, but they eventually learn that the last number counted represents the whole, an abstract concept.
- **The abstraction rule:** Not just numbers can be counted. Any object can be counted, whether it be the number of times bouncing a ball, the number of stuffed animals a child owns, etc. You can also count the lack of an object. If you have a tennis ball can with only two balls in it, you can count the missing ball as one.

Not all students naturally think abstractly. But how do we get them to do so using technology and math? One way to do this is through the use of manipulatives. Manipulatives are "items you can touch and move around that allow a student to count, figure out fractions, discern patterns, and other math tasks" (Stanley, 2018, p. 176). Manipulatives include blocks, shapes, base ten blocks, Unifix cubes, fraction bars, and plastic counting cubes. You can also use technology to create manipulatives. There are several digital manipulatives available for students, such as ST Math, which often requires students to manipulate objects in order to arrive at the correct answer, or visual manipulatives like tangrams, which represent physical objects.

Helping students to think abstractly, or develop outside-the-box thinking, will lead to more creativity and innovation. After all, anyone who thinks inside the box can only produce what is in that box. Those who are thinking outside of it can develop new ideas.

Crack the Code

In this project, students will create their own code for others to try to solve, complete with a clue to breaking the code and an answer key. Students can work either by themselves, in pairs, or in larger groups. The project must include: at least a three-digit code (can be more if students choose), a clue to figure out how to break the code, and an answer key.

When students or groups are finished, host a code-breaking challenge. Have students display their codes without the answer key for a gallery walk. Have students rotate around the room, moving from code to code, attempting to crack each code. Students should record their answers on a sheet of paper, making sure to match their guess with the number of each code. Once everyone has had a chance to attempt all of the codes, the code makers will put out their answer keys. Students will go around and check their answers against the keys, indicating how many they got correct. The person or team who breaks the most codes wins the challenge.

Materials

- ▸ Project Outline: Crack the Code (student copies)
- ▸ Suggested Timeline
- ▸ Lesson: How Can Numbers Represent Other Things?
- ▸ Lesson: How Do You Create a Code?
- ▸ Handout 5.1: Solving a Cryptogram (student copies)
- ▸ Handout 5.2: Testing Your Code (student copies)
- ▸ Product Rubric: Crack the Code (student copies)

PROJECT OUTLINE

Crack the Code

Big Idea

Abstract numbers can have practical uses.

Essential Question

How do you determine what numbers mean based on a pattern?

Deliverables

You will create your own code for others to try to solve, complete with a clue to breaking the code and an answer key.

Constraints

Your code must include:
▸ at least three digits,
▸ a clue to break it, and
▸ an answer key.

SUGGESTED TIMELINE

DAY				
1 Introduce the project and conduct Lesson: How Can Numbers Represent Other Things? *Ask.*	**2** Conduct Lesson: How Do You Create a Code? *Imagine/ Plan.*	**3** Have students create their own codes. *Create.*	**4** Have students test their codes with three different peers (see Handout 5.2). *Improve.*	**5** Host a code-breaking challenge.

How Can Numbers Represent Other Things?

1. Ask students: *When does a number not stand for a number? What about television channels?* Explain: *The number actually means the channel. If channel 18 is the Disney Channel, 18 stands for the Disney Channel. In sports, a number represents an athlete. For instance, number 23 is associated with LeBron James. The number of a license plate allows the police to look up who owns a car and if there are any previous violations. The numbers 0 and 1 stand for computer code, depending on the sequence they are placed in and how many there are.*

2. Tell students: *A number could stand for an important day. If I give the number 12/25, that stands for Christmas. We association the number with the date. A number could stand for a rating. The number 1 is the smallest number when looked at as a number, but if you tell someone they are number 1, you are saying they are the best. Seven numbers strung together represents someone's telephone number, and by putting them in the correct sequence, you can call them.*

3. Either as a class, in groups, or individually, have students solve a cryptogram where letters stands for numbers (see Handout 5.1). (*Note.* The solution is "The fall is the best time to pick a pumpkin.")

Project 5: Use Technology, Math, and Reasoning

How Do You Create a Code?

1. Tell students: *People can use numbers to create codes. By figuring out what the numbers represent, you can figure out what the numbers are trying to tell you. Consider the code of A1Z26, which is a very simple code. There are 26 letters in the English alphabet, so Z = 26 because it is the 26th letter in the alphabet. For example:*

A	B	C	D	E	F	G	H	I	J	K	L	M
1	2	3	4	5	6	7	8	9	10	11	12	13

N	O	P	Q	R	S	T	U	V	W	X	Y	Z
14	15	16	17	18	19	20	21	22	23	24	25	26

2. Ask: *If someone gave you the following code, what would it stand for using this system?* Have students determine what 4-15-7 means. (The answer is DOG because 4 = D, 15 = O, and 7 = G).

3. Ask: *How do you make your own code?* Tell students they need to determine what the numbers mean and then provide a clue so that someone can figure it out. For instance, if someone gave the number sequence of 1-0-5, and then provided the clue, "You might find a pot of gold at the end of one," students might guess that it has to do with a rainbow. If they go by the order of the colors of the rainbow, R-O-Y-G-B-I-V, 1 = red and 5 = blue.

4. Explain: *Then, it would take a little thinking to figure out what the 0 stands for. One might associate 0 with the lack of color because there is no 0 in the rainbow order. And the lack of hue would stand for white. The answer to the code would be red, white, and blue, like the American flag.*

Project 5: Use Technology, Math, and Reasoning

HANDOUT 5.1

Solving a Cryptogram

Directions: Solve the cryptogram. If you get stuck, the following hints may help you:

1. Single-letter words will likely be "a" or "I."

2. Repeated use of the same three-letter word may mean it is the word "the."

3. In all words, one letter must be a vowel (can sometimes be Y).

4. Certain consonants occur together, such as "th," "wh," "sh," and "ch." Consonants at the end of a word may indicate common endings, such as "-ing" or "-ed."

5. 16 has been used for P.

6. 11 has been used for K.

7. If you get stuck, read the puzzle and let your mind fill in the blanks. Sometimes you do not need the entire word to figure out the sentence.

Handout 5.1: Solving a Cryptogram, *continued*

Cryptogram

A	B	C	D	E	F	G	H	I	J	K	L	M

N	O	P	Q	R	S	T	U	V	W	X	Y	Z

___ ___ ___   ___ ___ ___ ___   ___ ___
20 8 5   6 1 12 12   9 19

___ ___ ___   ___ ___ ___ ___   ___ ___ ___ ___
20 8 5   2 5 19 20   20 9 13 5

___ ___   ___ ___ ___ ___   ___
20 15   16 9 3 11   1

___ ___ ___ ___ ___ ___ ___
16 21 13 16 11 9 14

Project 5: Use Technology, Math, and Reasoning

HANDOUT 5.2

Testing Your Code

Directions: Test your code with three different peers. Try to solve each other's codes. Then, work to revise your code as needed.

1. Review how easy or how difficult it was for each of your partners to decipher your code.

2. If it was too easy, you might want to make your code a little more challenging.

3. If it was too difficult, you might want to offer additional clues to make the solving of your code easier.

4. If it was a challenge but not too difficult, you can leave your code the way it is.

5. Have your revised code ready to go for the next class along with its answer key.

PRODUCT RUBRIC

Crack the Code

	Code	Answer Key
Great	The code is more than three digits long. The code is presented in a creative manner.	The clue provided is challenging, but the code can be solved. The answer key unlocks the clue and clearly links to the clue.
Good	The code is three digits long. The code is presented in a plain manner that meets the requirements.	The clue provided is challenging, but it is almost too difficult for someone to figure out. The answer key unlocks the clue but cannot be clearly linked to the clue.
Needs Improvement	The code is less than three digits long. The code is too messy to read or is confusing.	The clue provided is so challenging that the code cannot be solved using it. The answer key is either wrong, very unclear, or not provided.

6 Use and Analyze Models

Models bring ideas and concepts to life, making them more practical and easier to understand. We use models a lot in the STEM world. How many students create their own volcano or make a Styrofoam version of the solar system in science class in order to better understand these concepts? Think about architects and structural engineers. When they develop a new building, they do not build the actual structure at first. They construct a model of it so that they can test it and understand what problems need to be addressed before moving on to the actual structure. A perfect example of this would be the Shanghai World Financial Center. In its first designs and model stage, there was a circular opening near the top of the 1,600-foot tall structure to reduce the stresses of wind pressure. However, when architects created the model, they understood the difficulty and expense of making the shape circular. Buildings typically use straight lines in their construction because they are more practical and easier to work with. Because of this, they changed the shape to that of a trapezoid.

Most importantly, models allow us access that we might not have otherwise. We cannot take a student into the center of Earth in order to experience its layers. Not only is this impractical from the standpoint of getting permission slips and liability waivers, it is impossible to dig that deep or survive the molten outer core of our planet. However, we can analyze a model of the Earth that shows the different layers, helping students to see something they normally would not be able to see. It would also be challenging to take someone's skull off and poke around in his or her brain in order to understand how it works. But a plastic version of the human brain with removable parts allows someone unlimited access to learn about the brain's structure without risk.

Would students rather read about the rainforest in a book or create a version of the biome complete with producers, consumers, and resources? Would students rather look at photos of the Eiffel Tower or create their own out of toothpicks? Wouldn't it be so much more fun to create a model of New York City that shows the coordinate plane rather than sketching out lines on a worksheet? Models make learning both engaging and authentic. Students learn more through such hands-on activities and actually produce something that others are going to see on display.

Analyzing models also leads to greater understanding. Meteorologists study models of hurricanes in order to try to predict what path one might actually take. Mathematicians spend a lifetime studying models, trying to crack the code that will lead to a new mathematical concept. Engineers study models of new cars and how they react to resistance in wind tunnels to shape the final design of the vehicle. When students create models, they can then analyze other students' models to gain a better understanding. Rather than have each student create a model of the human body, have each student take a different part of the human body and create a more detailed model. If you have 20 students in the classrooms, you could have 20 different body parts. When you go to display, set up the classroom like a human body, the brain being at the top, the heart or stomach being in the middle, with the feet being at the bottom. Students can walk around this giant human body, learning about different parts and organs and what they do for the body.

Models are a practical way to study large concepts, and best of all, they bring learning to life. Students are able to interact and study the models so that they see how abstract concepts actually look and function.

Where in the World Is Your Neighborhood?

In this project, students will create a map of their neighborhood, including landmarks, streets names, and other features found on most maps, such as stores, public buildings, playgrounds or other sports fields, or physical features that remain permanent. Students' maps may be made of anything they choose, but an explanation or legend must be provided. When students have completed their maps, have students display them. As a class, try to piece together the various parts of the town you live in. There will probably be some overlap, but see if you can show the neighborhood surrounding the school.

Materials

- ▶ Paper and other supplies (for student maps)
- ▶ Project Outline: Where in the World Is Your Neighborhood? (student copies)
- ▶ Suggested Timeline
- ▶ Lesson: How Well Do You Know Your Neighborhood?
- ▶ Lesson: What Are the Different Types of Maps?
- ▶ Lesson: What Makes a Map Look Professional?
- ▶ Handout 6.1: How Does a Key on a Map Work? (student copies)
- ▶ Product Rubric: Where in the World Is Your Neighborhood? (student copies)

PROJECT OUTLINE

Where in the World Is Your Neighborhood?

Big Idea

How well do you know your neighborhood?

Essential Question

How does someone create a map?

Deliverables

You will create a map of your neighborhood. You will include things such as land-marks, streets names, and other features. The map may be made of anything you choose, but an explanation or legend must be provided.

You will need to research your neighborhood in order to determine its features. The research can come in many forms. You can:

- ▸ use a computer program such as Google Earth or Google Maps,
- ▸ walk around your neighborhood with a parent and make note of the different features on your street,
- ▸ try to recall from memory the features in your neighborhood, and/or
- ▸ interview a family member about the features in your neighborhood.

The features you are specifically looking for are:

- ▸ the address of your residence,
- ▸ the immediate street your residence is on,
- ▸ at least one other cross street (although you can include more than one),
- ▸ at least five landmarks in the area (e.g., other houses, water tower, businesses, schools), and
- ▸ the sizes of the landmarks.

Constraints

Your map must include:

- ▸ at least two streets,
- ▸ at least five landmarks, and
- ▸ your address.

SUGGESTED TIMELINE

DAY				
1 Introduce the project and conduct Lesson: How Well Do You Know Your Neighborhood? *Ask.*	**2** Conduct Lesson: What Are the Different Types of Maps? *Ask.*	**3** Have students explore map keys (see Handout 6.1). *Ask.*	**4** Have students research their neighborhoods, writing down street names, landmarks, and other features. *Plan.*	**5** Have students continue to research their neighborhoods. *Plan.*
6 Have students bring information about their neighborhoods and begin rough draft of their maps. *Create.*	**7** Conduct Lesson: What Makes a Map Look Professional? *Improve.*	**8** Have students begin working on their final drafts. *Improve.*	**9** Have students continue to work on their final drafts. *Improve.*	**10** Have students display their maps for the class. Try to piece together the community.

How Well Do You Know Your Neighborhood?

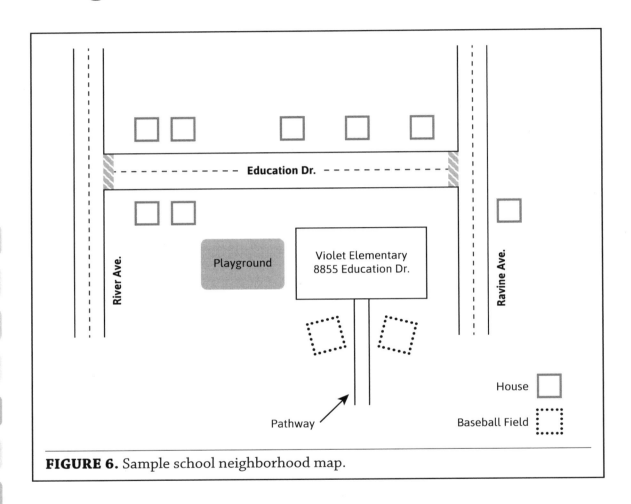

FIGURE 6. Sample school neighborhood map.

1. As a class, draw a map of the school on the board. This map should include:
   ▸ the street name the school is on,
   ▸ a representation of the school,
   ▸ any intersecting streets, and
   ▸ any landmarks or features.

2. Try to see how far the class can expand the map, adding more and more detail to it (see Figure 6).

What Are the Different Types of Maps?

1. Tell students that different maps feature different objects depending on the purpose of the map. There are many different types of maps. The three most common ones are:
   ▸ a political map, which shows how land is used by people,
   ▸ a physical map, which shows the shape of the land, and
   ▸ a road map, which shows the roads available for people to use.

2. Share with students an example of a political map. Many are available online, such as http://www.emapsworld.com/usa-political-map.html. Consider also displaying a political map of the local town/city, and/or have students locate such a map. Ask: *Why do you think political maps are important?*

3. Explain that political maps help viewers determine where man-made boundaries have been drawn, such as boundaries of cities, townships, counties, and states. These maps help people understand where one territory ends and another begins.

4. Share with students an example of a physical map of the United States, such as http://maps.maphill.com/united-states/maps/physical-map/physical-map-of-united-states.jpg. Ask: *What do you notice about this map?*

5. Guide students to understand that physical maps help viewers understand the terrain of an area, including natural features and elevation. This helps because it shows people where they can build or travel.

6. Ask students to look closely at the physical map of the U.S. The large brown area is full of mountains. Explain that there are not a whole lot of people living in those areas compared to other parts of the country because it is difficult to build a house on a mountain. You often need flatter ground.

7. Tell students that physical maps also let viewers see where bodies of water are. Again, this helps in understanding where or where not to place certain structures.

8. Share with students an example of a road map, such as http://ontheworldmap.com/usa/usa-road-map.jpg. Explain that road maps show all of the man-made roads available to people to use for driving. Road maps are helpful for traveling almost anywhere—whether it's a cross-country trip or an outing to a new grocery store.

9. Ask: *What type of map are we going to use for our map of the neighborhood?* (A road map.) Ask: *Why do you think that is the best map for our purposes?*

What Makes a Map Look Professional?

1. Ask students: *When you look at a map, what is the most important thing?*
2. Tell students: *The most important thing is that you can tell what is on the map. One way to make a map easier to read is by making it as professional as possible.*
3. Display a professional map and ask students to point out what about it looks professional.
4. Share with students several suggestions for making their maps look as professional as possible. They can:
   ▸ use blank paper or graph paper,
   ▸ use a ruler to draw straight lines,
   ▸ use a glass or a compass to draw circles,
   ▸ use color to make it more vibrant, and/or
   ▸ design it on a computer.

5. Remind students: *You will want to take the information you have gathered, including rough drafts of your map, and make a final, clean version of your neighborhood map.*

HANDOUT 6.1

How Does a Key on a Map Work?

Directions: All maps have keys. These keys let viewers know what symbols stand for. Depending on a map's key, one symbol on one map might mean one thing, while on a different map it could stand for something else. You will want to make sure to let people know what the different symbols on your map mean.

Practice working with the key for the map on the following page. Use crayons to properly label the map using the key.

1. Color the river blue.

2. Circle the hospital with red.

3. Draw a straight green line from the police station to the school.

4. Color the sewage line brown.

5. Draw an orange line from the airport to the city hall using the roads.

Handout 6.1: How Does a Key on a Map Work?, *continued*

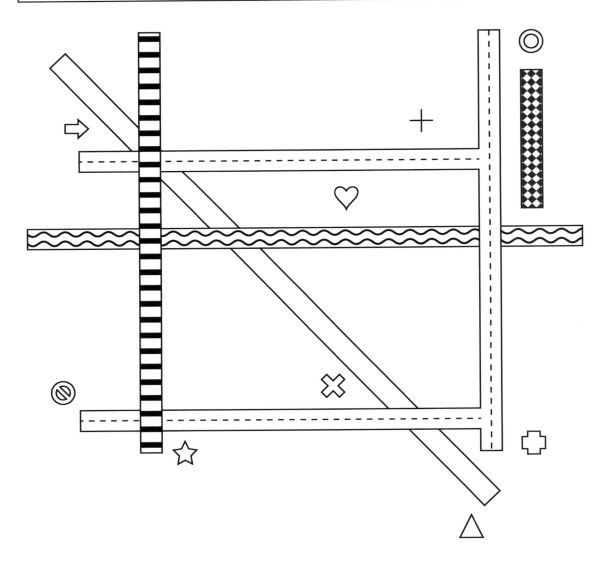

Project 6: Use and Analyze Models

Name: _____ Date: _____

PRODUCT RUBRIC

Where in the World Is Your Neighborhood?

	Requirements	Map
Great	The map not only meets all five requirements but also goes above and beyond them by providing more details. A detailed explanation or a clear legend is provided.	The map is very creative, bringing the neighborhood to life. The map is created in a professional manner, making it easy to read and tell what symbols represent.
Good	The map meets the five basic requirements. An explanation or a legend is provided, but it is not completely clear.	You can tell which neighborhood the map is trying to represent, but it is not really brought to life. The map can be read, but there are a few places where it looks unprofessional.
Needs Improvement	The map meets the five basic requirements. Neither an explanation nor a legend is provided.	It is difficult to tell which neighborhood the map is trying to represent; it does not look like a neighborhood. The map is very sloppy and unprofessional.

7 Record and Analyze Data

One of the most important things STEM professionals must do while conducting an experiment or research is to record the data they collect. This is because they are following the engineering design process and they wish to replicate their results, they need to keep track of what they did.

Recording data over time can be a valuable tool. We do this with students, recording grades and evaluations over the course of the year to determine whether the student is ready to move on to the next level. We use this data to adjust our teaching and ensure that students get what they need in the classroom, so we are constantly analyzing the data to inform our decisions. We record data in the form of memories and use it to make decisions all of the time. For example, if a person goes to a restaurant and receives bad service, he or she is probably going to be hesitant to return. If the person does go back and feels treated badly a second time, it is very unlikely this person will ever eat at this restaurant again. Businesses analyze data to predict what they need to do in order to turn a profit. They look at the history of sales and how the market is trending. They then try to predict whether the trends will continue, or they can make changes to try to increase profits.

The key is to organize data so that it can be understood and interpreted. Students need to be shown what organizational tools are at their disposal and then decide which ones will best display their data. The best graphic organizer to use is the one that will allow anyone to access and understand the data. That means properly labeling and having a key so that others can understand what the data are showing.

Organizing data is a good skill for students, especially gifted ones, to learn and practice. Students sometimes have grandiose notions but cannot funnel them into a form that can be shared and reflected on with others. Learning how to do this will lead to more purposeful reflection. Through reflection, the most valuable learning takes place. There is sometimes a difference between what you want students to learn and what they actually learn. And each student might have a different takeaway from a lesson or activity. It is important to create space where students can reflect upon their own learning. Sometimes students do this through portfolios in which they build a collect of their own work over the course of a semester or year. To make a portfolio meaningful, students need to analyze how or if they have grown over the course of the year. This is where that reflection takes place. Whenever students are looking at data over time, there needs to be an opportunity for them to reflect upon what was learned.

How Far Will It Fly?

In this project, students will work in groups to design and construct three paper airplane designs and fly them to see which of the designs is the most aerodynamic. Through trial and error, students will compare and contrast the results of each flight. They will then determine which design is the most successful.

Students can reflect on one or more of the following topics. These reflections can be written, in a discussion, or paired and shared:

- ▸ Do you think it was important for everyone in the group to have a specific role? What advantages did it provide? What were the disadvantages?
- ▸ Did your group work well together? If they did, why do you suppose this was? If not, why do you think that was?

- ▶ If you had a choice to work on this project by yourself or with a group, which would you choose and why?
- ▶ Why do you suppose it is important to learn how to work in a group? How often do you think you will need to work in groups when you are older?
- ▶ What could your group have done to have worked better together and produced a better project?

Materials

- ▶ Project Outline: How Far Will It Fly? (student copies)
- ▶ Suggested Timeline
- ▶ Lesson: Setting Up the Experiment
- ▶ Lesson: What Is a Variable?
- ▶ Lesson: Graphing Data
- ▶ Handout 7.1: Which Plane Will Fly the Farthest? (student copies)
- ▶ Handout 7.2: Flight Record Data (student copies)
- ▶ Product Rubric: How Far Will It Fly? (student copies)

PROJECT OUTLINE

How Far Will It Fly?

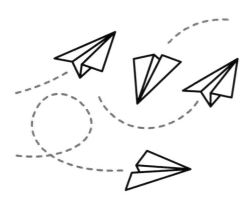

Big Idea

Comparing and contrasting results can lead to improvement and reveal successes.

Essential Question

How do you record and analyze data?

Deliverables

You will work with a team to design, construct, and fly paper airplanes to see which of the designs is the most aerodynamic. Through trial and error, you will record the flights of these planes and compare them against each other. You will then determine which design is the most successful by comparing and contrasting your results.

Constraints

Your plane designs:
▸ must feature three different designs,
▸ must use the same material,
▸ must have the same person fly them.

SUGGESTED TIMELINE

DAY				
1 Introduce the project and conduct Lesson: Setting Up the Experiment. *Ask.*	**2** Have students work in teams to plan their projects. *Imagine.*	**3** Have teams do background research to determine which three planes they are going to use and make a guess as to which will fly the farthest. *Plan.*	**4** Conduct Lesson: What Is a Variable? Have teams begin constructing their airplanes. *Ask.*	**5** Have teams create Plane 1 and test it. *Create.*
6 Have teams create Plane 2 and test it. *Create.*	**7** Have teams create Plane 3 and test it. *Create.*	**8** Conduct Lesson: Graphic Data. Have teams show the distances flown in feet and inches on a line plot. *Create.*	**9** Have teams report their findings, using the data to support the conclusion and compare it to their guess. *Improve.*	**10** Have teams compete against each other, putting forth their best plane to determine a class champion.

Project 7: Record and Analyze Data

LESSON

Setting Up the Experiment

1. Use paper airplane designs (available online; search for "paper airplane designs") to create three paper airplanes. Label the planes 1–3. Present the designs to the class and have students guess which one they think will fly the farthest. Distribute Handout 7.1 for students to record their responses throughout this lesson. Use the following questions in order to spark discussion about the experiment:
   - Which do you think will fly the farthest?
   - Why did you pick the plane you did?
   - Would it be more valid just to fly each plane once or multiple times? Why?
   - What could affect the outcome of the experiment?

2. Ask: *How many of me (the teacher) do you think it will take to measure the distance each plane flew?* Have students make their guesses as to how many of your body lengths each plane will fly.

3. Then, fly each of the three designs. Measure the distances, and have students record their responses on Handout 7.1. Continue the discussion:
   - Were you correct in your guess?
   - Why do you think the plane that went the farthest did so?
   - Was your estimation of how many body lengths it would fly correct?
   - Why do you suppose your guess was either correct or not?

4. Afterward, explain to students that they will be completing a similar experiment in groups, where they will fly three planes, trying to guess which they believe will go the farthest.

What Is a Variable?

1. Tell students: *Variables are conditions that can affect the outcome of an experiment. Good scientists try to eliminate as many variables as possible from their experiments so that they are getting the most accurate results.*

2. Tell students that an example of a variable could be the paper they use to build their planes. Perhaps the paper for each plane is a different thickness. To eliminate this variable, they would want to make the paper airplanes with the same thickness of paper.

3. Ask: *What would be some other examples of a variable in your project?* Students may consider variables, such as:
   ▸ The same person doesn't throw all of the planes.
   ▸ The person throwing the planes throws some harder than others.
   ▸ The person doesn't use the same throwing technique with all of the planes.
   ▸ The person gets tired halfway through the experiment.
   ▸ Some planes are thrown indoors, while others are thrown outdoors.
   ▸ One plane is made better than another.
   ▸ One plane has its folds taped down while another does not.
   ▸ You use different measuring tools to measure the distance.
   ▸ You are not accurate in your measurement.
   ▸ You lose half of your data and have to do that part of the experiment again.

4. Have students begin constructing their planes. Distribute Handout 7.2 for students to record their data as they work.

Project 7: Record and Analyze Data

LESSON

Graphing Data

1. Explain to students that they are going to take the data they have collected and organize it on a line plot for each of their three planes.
2. Review with students the following steps for graphing data on a line plot:
   ▸ Step #1: Gather your data. In this case you have already done this in the experiment you ran with flying the planes.
   ▸ Step #2: Organize your data in some kind of order, such as by the type of plane and the number of the flight.
   ▸ Step #3: Create a horizontal line.

⟵――⟶

   ▸ Step #4: Make a mark above the horizontal line each time data occur.

Flight #1:   X

Flight #2:   X

Flight #3:   X

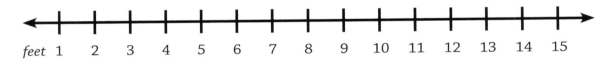

feet 1   2   3   4   5   6   7   8   9   10   11   12   13   14   15

   ▸ Step #5: Interpret the data. In this example, Flight #3 flew the farthest and Flight #2 the shortest.

3. Using Handout 7.2, have students complete line plots for each of their planes.

HANDOUT 7.1

Which Plane Will Fly the Farthest?

Directions: Consider the three planes your teacher has presented to you. Then, answer the following questions.

1. Which plane do you think will fly the farthest? Circle your response.

    Plane #1   Plane #2   Plane #3

2. Why do you think it will fly farther than the others?

3. Record the distance each plane flew.

	Plane #1	**Plane #2**	**Plane #3**
Flight #1			
Flight #2			
Flight #3			

4. Was your initial guess correct? Circle your response

    Yes   No

Project 7: Record and Analyze Data

HANDOUT 7.2

Flight Record Data

Directions: Use this worksheet to record data about each of your flights.

Plane #1 Design: _____
Flight Distances (in feet):

Flight #1: _____   Flight #2: _____   Flight #3: _____

Plane #2 Design: _____
Flight Distances (in feet):

Flight #1: _____   Flight #2: _____   Flight #3: _____

Plane #3 Design: _____
Flight Distances (in feet):

Flight #1: _____   Flight #2: _____   Flight #3: _____

Flight Line Plots

Complete a line plot for each of your plane's flights.

Handout 7.2: Flight Record Data, *continued*

Plane #1:

Flight #1:

Flight #2:

Flight #3:

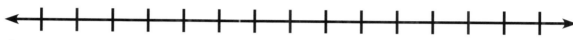

feet

Plane #2:

Flight #1:

Flight #2:

Flight #3:

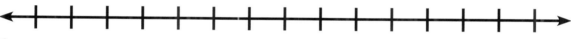

feet

Plane #3:

Flight #1:

Flight #2:

Flight #3:

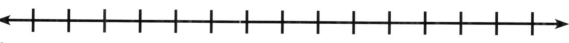

feet

Which plane was the most successful? Why?

Project 7: Record and Analyze Data

Name: _____   Date: _____

PRODUCT RUBRIC

How Far Will It Fly?

	Data	**Groupwork**
Great	Flight record data are well-organized, and the results on the line plot are clear. Data are labeled correctly; results are accurate and easy to understand.	Student contributed to his or her part of the experiment as well as other parts. Student made him- or herself a valuable member of the group by offering positive contributions to the group dynamic.
Good	Data are well-organized for the most part, but there are a couple of places where the results are unclear. Data are mostly labeled correctly, making results accurate and easy to understand, but a couple of areas are unclear.	Student contributed to his or her part of the experiment but not a lot for other parts. Student made him- or herself a valuable member of the group most of the time by offering positive contributions to the group dynamic, but there were a few times when he or she was negative or a distraction.
Needs Improvement	Data are not well-organized, making it difficult to tell what the results were. Data are mislabeled in a lot of places, making results inaccurate and difficult to understand.	Student did not even contribute to his or her part of the experiment. Student did not contribute positively to the group dynamic, oftentimes being negative or a distraction.

Project 7: Record and Analyze Data

8 Investigate Change Over Time and Patterns

One of the most valuable things you can teach students is that history repeats itself. Consider World War I and World War II, the assassinations of Abraham Lincoln and John F. Kennedy, and the fall of the Greek and Roman Empires. Students may wonder, "How do you avoid history repeating itself?" The answer is: by learning from it. By studying patterns and trends, students can make educated predictions. Consider global warming and climate change. Scientists have noticed a trend that the world is getting warmer, as pollution destroys the ozone a little bit every year. As a result of this pattern, humans are working to combat climate change by cutting down on emissions that cause this deterioration.

Patterns are evident in the advancement of technology, with a new iPhone coming out each year, computers getting smaller and smarter, and self-driving cars becoming more commonplace. It is the study of these advances in technology that leads to further advancements. We are constantly trying to make things better. It is human nature. By studying changes over time, we are able to determine what we do not need anymore, what we need to continue to do, and what we need to add to improve something.

In the classroom, we do not have the luxury of studying something firsthand over a long period of time. But we can run an experiment for a few weeks, chart observations over a limited period of time, run a brief investigation of what may happen, and study the past to determine how elements change over time.

What Do You See in the Clouds?

In this project, students will create a model of a cloud configuration they find interesting using cotton balls. In order to construct their models, students should spend some time outside over a 5-day period to look at the clouds (or photos of clouds should outside access not be available). Each day, students should document what they observe during each trip outside in a journal (i.e., in a notebook, on a piece of paper, or on an electronic device) using a combination of written sentences and drawings:

- **Journal #1:** What did you see in the clouds today? Did you notice any patterns?
- **Journal #2:** What did you see in the clouds today? Did you notice any patterns? Do you see any similar patterns from the day before?
- **Journal #3:** What did you see in the clouds today? Did you notice any patterns? Do you see any similar patterns from the day before?
- **Journal #4:** What did you see in the clouds today? Did you notice any patterns? Do you see any similar patterns from the day before?
- **Journal #5:** What did you see in the clouds today? Did you notice any patterns? Do you see any similar patterns from the day before?

After the 5 days, students should consider the most interesting thing they saw in the clouds and reenact it using cotton balls. This might be a pattern, an object, a shape, a person, an animal, or a symbol, etc. Students should be provided with cotton balls and a piece of construction paper to glue the cotton balls to. They will need to manipulate the cotton balls into the shape they saw and journaled about. They will then display their cloud representations for the class.

Materials

- ▶ Cotton balls, glue, and construction paper (for each student)
- ▶ Project Outline: What Do You See in the Clouds? (student copies)
- ▶ Suggested Timeline
- ▶ Lesson: What Are Clouds?
- ▶ Product Rubric: What Do You See in the Clouds? (student copies)

PROJECT OUTLINE

What Do You See in the Clouds?

Big Idea

People can observe the same thing and have different interpretations.

Essential Question

What do you notice about changes in patterns in the clouds over time?

Deliverables

Using cotton balls, you will create a model of the cloud configuration you find most interesting. You will observe cloud formations for 5 days, recording what you see in a journal. In your journal entries, you will answer the questions: *What did you see in the clouds today? Did you notice any patterns? Do you see any similar patterns from the day before?* After the 5 days, you will recreate your favorite cloud pattern that you observed and then display it for the class.

Constraints

You must use cotton balls.

SUGGESTED TIMELINE

DAY				
1 Introduce the project and conduct Lesson: What Are Clouds? *Ask.*	**2** Have students continue to observe the clouds and journal. *Imagine.*	**3** Have students continue to observe the clouds and journal. *Imagine.*	**4** Have students continue to observe the clouds and journal. *Imagine.*	**5** Have students continue to observe the clouds and journal. *Imagine.*
6 Have students continue to observe the clouds and journal. *Imagine.*	**7** Have students plan their cloud representations. *Plan.*	**8** Have students create their cloud representations. *Create.*	**9** Have students complete their cloud representations. *Improve.*	**10** Have students display their cloud representations.

What Are Clouds?

1. Tell students: *Clouds are made up of water droplets or ice crystals. These are so small they are able to float in the air. These water droplets and ice crystals form when water from the ground evaporates and turns into water vapor. As it floats in the air, it attaches itself to dust or pollen in the sky and forms clouds.*
2. Introduce students to three cloud shapes (many photos are available online):
   ▸ cirrus, which look like feathers;
   ▸ cumulus, which look like cotton balls; and
   ▸ stratus, which look like bed sheets.

3. Tell students: *Clouds can sometimes create patterns that cause them to look like something other than a cloud. This could be a definitive shape, such as a heart or square, an object such as a car, or an animal or person.*
4. Take students outside and find a good place to look at the sky. Make sure it is a day where there are actual clouds. Ask students to look for patterns in the clouds.
5. As a class, discuss which shapes students can see in the clouds, comparing what one student may see in a specific cloud pattern to what another student sees.
6. Over the next 5 days, take students outside to look at the sky and look for new patterns and shapes. Students should record their observations in a notebook or on a piece of paper.

Name: _____ Date: _____

PRODUCT RUBRIC

What Do You See in the Clouds?

	Journal	Cloud
Great	Student has all five journal entries. All journal entries are detailed, allowing the reader to see what the student saw.	The object the student saw is clearly represented by the cotton balls. Cloud artwork is done neatly; it appears the student spent some time on it.
Good	Student has five journal entries, but they are incomplete. The journal entries have some detail that allows the reader to see what the student saw, but not all of the time.	The object the student saw is represented by the cotton balls, but it is not completely clear. Cloud artwork is done well but could have been neater, or the student could have spent more time on it.
Needs Improvement	Student has less than five journal entries. Journal entries lack detail, making it hard for the reader to see what the student saw.	The object the student saw is not clearly represented by the cotton balls. Cloud artwork is done sloppily; it looks like the student did not spend much time on it.

9 Use Computer Models or Simulations

As technology becomes more and more prevalent in education, so, too, does the issue of using it properly. Technology, like any tool, is only effective if it improves learning. There are several ways to use technology to enhance the learning of students, but one that is especially effective is the use of computer models, which allow students to ask "What if . . . ?" What if this happened instead of that, what if this had never happened, or what if we did it differently? Computer models allow students to try their solution in different ways. They can make three or four attempts at something, changing something major or just making minor tweaks, leading them closer and closer to a functional solution. Computer models allow students to fail with a safety net in place. If a student is making a model out of popsicle sticks only to find out halfway through that he made a mistake in his foundation, he would have to throw the entire thing out and start with new materials.

The computer program *Sim City* is an excellent example. You can build entire cities, including infrastructure, buildings, and other items crucial to the success of a city. The program alerts you if your city is not performing like it should. If you do not string enough electricity throughout the city, there are homes and businesses that will be without electricity. This makes it difficult for them to be successful. If you put the fire department on one side of town only to have a fire break out on the complete opposite side, by the time the fire truck gets to its destination, the building will have burned down. If the town becomes too unhappy, you start to lose residents, and when that happens, you lose money needed to keep building. If you have enough problems with the city, you can simply hit the destruct button and bring the whole thing to the ground and start all over again.

How many times were you playing a video game, such as *Donkey Kong*, only to either be hit by a barrel, caught on fire by a fireball, or have the bouncy thing land on your head? When failure happened, what did you do? You put another quarter in the slot and tried again. You would try and fail for hours on end. Nowadays with Microsoft Xbox, Nintendo Switch, and Sony PlayStation, simply pushing a button allows you to try again. This process is all about learning—learning what you did wrong, learning what not to do, learning what works. This is the sort of resilience we should bring into the classroom.

Computer simulations make problem solving more authentic because they put students in the shoes of the person or people experiencing the problem, and they are also excellent examples of learning from failure. Using computer simulations and models to teach students that failure is okay encourages students to take risks. Taking a risk is where the most learning takes place. This is the power technology can have in the classroom.

What If There Were No Light Bulb?

In this project, students will study an important invention and create a simulation using an online animation program that will show how the world would be different without this invention.

Materials

- ▶ Read aloud about inventing, such as *So You Want to Be an Inventor?* by Judith St. George
- ▶ Project Outline: What If There Were No Light Bulb? (student copies)

- ▶ Suggested Timeline
- ▶ Lesson: What Are the Most Important Inventions Ever?
- ▶ Lesson: What Would Life Look Like If We Took Away the Light Bulb?
- ▶ Handout 9.1: An Important Invention (student copies)
- ▶ Product Rubric: What If There Were No Light Bulb? (student copies)

PROJECT OUTLINE

What If There Were No Light Bulb?

Big Idea

There is a positive ripple effect when a new innovation comes along.

Essential Question

What would the world look like without a particular invention? How would things be different?

Deliverables

Take an important invention and create a simulation using an online animation program that will show how the world would be different without this invention. Your simulation should show someone in the present day who does not have access to the invention you chose, and how this person's life is different from yours. Some online animation programs to consider include Book Creator, Powtoon, Toontastic 3D, Puppet Pals HD, Storybird, and Google Slides.

Your story must have:
▶ a main character;
▶ a beginning, middle, and end; and
▶ three scenes of how this person's life is different without the invention you chose, one at the beginning, one at the middle, and one at the end.

You may add other characters, more than three ways life would be different, and/or more details to your story.

Constraints

Your animation must:
▶ tell a story,
▶ be developed using an online animation program, and
▶ include three ways the world would be different without the invention.

SUGGESTED TIMELINE

DAY				
1 Introduce project and conduct Lesson: What Are the Most Important Inventions Ever? *Ask.*	**2** Conduct Lesson: What Would Life Look Like If We Took Away the Light Bulb? *Imagine.*	**3** Have students pick an invention they think is important (see Handout 9.1). *Ask.*	**4** Have students research their selected inventions. *Ask.*	**5** Have students choose how they are going to present their scenarios. *Plan.*
6 Have students work on their products. *Plan/ Create.*	**7** Have students work on their products. *Create.*	**8** Have students work on their products. *Create.*	**9** Have student finalize and revise their products. *Improve.*	**10** Have students present their simulations.

What Are the Most Important Inventions Ever?

1. Read to students *So You Want to Be an Inventor?* by Judith St. George. Then, have a whole-class discussion about some of the inventions mentioned in the book.

2. Engage students in a class debate. Have them try to list some of the most important inventions ever. They should be able to explain why they think each invention is so important. Some of these inventions might include computers, WiFi, bathtubs, cell phones, beds, electricity, iPads, the Internet, cars, money, light bulbs, etc.

3. Suggest some inventions students might not think of, such as the compass, the printing press, books, paper, Penicillin, internal combustion engines, airplanes, the wheel, and the television, and discuss why they might be considered important. You might find that students can talk about inventions for hours!

What Would Life Look Like If We Took Away the Light Bulb?

1. Ask students to play a "What if . . .?" game about an invention that they use daily and take for granted—the light bulb. Ask them to imagine if this invention had never been invented.

2. Ask: *What are some things that the light bulb provides for us that are important?* Light bulbs:
    ▸   allow us to see better,
    ▸   allow us to work at night,
    ▸   provide safety to avoid hazards,
    ▸   provide warmth, and
    ▸   provided access to future inventions that use wiring and energy.

3. Ask: *What are some things that might be different if we had never invented the light bulb?* Ask the class to generate a list, but these are some things students might think about:
    ▸   People would not be able to do as many activities at night, such as read.
    ▸   Sports such as football and baseball would not be able to be played at night because there would be no stadium lights.
    ▸   There would be more air accidents because planes couldn't see the runway or other planes.
    ▸   People might not have computers, televisions, toasters, or anything that runs on electricity because without lights there would have been no reason to run electricity to houses.
    ▸   There would be more fires because people would be burning candles and oil, which can cause fires.

Project 9: Use Computer Models or Simulations

HANDOUT 9.1

An Important Invention

Directions: Consider inventions you think are important. Answer the following the questions.

1. What are three inventions that you feel are important?

2. Why do you feel each of these inventions is so important?

Project 9: Use Computer Models or Simulations

Handout 9.1: An Important Invention, *continued*

3. Either through research, talking to someone, or prior knowledge, list three important facts about each invention you listed.

	Invention 1	Invention 2	Invention 3
Facts			

4. Choose the invention of the most interest to you. Now imagine if you did not have this invention. What are three ways your life would be different? These will form your story.

Project 9: Use Computer Models or Simulations

PRODUCT RUBRIC

What If There Were No Light Bulb?

	Animation	Story
Great	There are more than three scenes animated. There is a clear beginning, middle, and end to the story.	The story contains a clear main character. How the world has changed due to the lack of this invention is logically explained.
Good	There are three scenes animated. There is a beginning, middle, and end to the story, but it is not obvious where one ends and the other begins.	The story contains a main character, but it is hard to figure out which one. How the world has changed due to the lack of this invention is explained but not always logically.
Needs improvement	There are less than three scenes animated. There is a not a beginning, middle, and end to the story, making it difficult to follow.	The story does not contain a main character. It either does not show how the world has changed due to the lack of this invention or has no logic as to how the world is different.

10 Construct and Explain Systems

Systems can be quite complicated. Take our political system, for example. A basic understanding of it is that there are three branches of government, each watching the other to make sure there is no abuse of power. In practice, we know it is far more complex than this. Because many systems are so complex, from ecosystems to the Earth's climate to the solar system, having the ability to analyze complicated systems and describe them concisely and accurately is a valuable skill.

We start small with students, asking them to understand ecosystems, how the economy works, systems of equations, or what system to use in order to write a clear essay. We ask students to explain systems, or write them, or to be able to explain them visually. By being able to understand a system, students are able to see both the big picture as well as the little details. Usually when people fail at systems, it is because they either do not see the big picture or do not understand how the details are put together to create it. Understanding systems is a valuable skill for students to possess indeed.

Everyone Is Playing It

In this project, students will create their own original sport, including a scoring system. They will also design a playing field with dimensions in the appropriate measurement. They must determine:

- how one wins,
- how one keeps score,
- how many people can play,
- how many teams can play,
- how large the playing field is,
- the length of a game and how it is timed,
- what equipment is used, and
- the rules.

They must then demonstrate how their sport is played. They must also demonstrate how math is used in the sport. There are three different options for how they display their sports:

- Level 1: Draw a diagram.
- Level 2: Create a 3-D model.
- Level 3: Perform a live demonstration or record a video.

On demonstration day, you should ideally provide a large presentation area, such as a gym, and have students set up their projects. There needs to be an area for students to display their Level 1 and Level 2 projects, and there needs to be space or technology available for students to present their Level 3 demonstrations.

Materials

- Project Outline: Everyone Is Playing It (student copies)
- Suggested Timeline
- Lesson: How Are Sports Organized?
- Lesson: How Is Math Used in Sports?
- Handout 10.1: Practice Day (student copies)
- Product Rubric: Everyone Is Playing It (student copies)

PROJECT OUTLINE

Everyone Is Playing It

Big Idea

Math is used in nearly every sport.

Essential Question

If you could create your very own sport, what would it look like?

Deliverables

You will create your own original sport, including a scoring system. You will also design a playing field with dimensions in the appropriate measurement. You must determine:

- how one wins,
- how one keeps score,
- how many people can play,
- how many teams can play,
- how large the playing field is,
- the length of a game and how it is timed,
- what equipment is used, and
- the rules.

You must then demonstrate how your sport is played. You must also demonstrate how math is used in the sport. There are three different options for how you display your sport:

- **Level 1:** Draw a diagram for how your sport would be played.
- **Level 2:** Create a 3-D model showing how your sport would be played.
- **Level 3:** Perform a live demonstration or record a video that shows how the sport is played.

Constraints

Your sport must:

- feature or include math in some way,
- be an original sport (not a version of an already existing sport), and
- be simple enough to demonstrate easily to others.

SUGGESTED TIMELINE

DAY				
1 Introduce project and conduct Lesson: How Are Sports Organized? *Ask.*	**2** Conduct Lesson: How Is Math Used in Sports? *Ask.*	**3** Have students imagine what their new sport will look like. *Imagine.*	**4** Have students plan how math will be involved in the sport. *Plan.*	**5** Have students begin rough drafts of their sports. *Plan.*
6 Have students continue to plan their sports. *Create.*	**7** Have students finalize how their sport is played. *Create.*	**8** Have students practice their sports demonstrations (see Handout 10.1). *Improve.*	**9** Have students make final revisions to their sports and presentations. *Improve.*	**10** Have students demonstrate their sports.

Project 10: Construct and Explain Systems

How Are Sports Organized?

1. Tell students that Ancient Mayans played a game very similar to soccer and basketball where they had to kick a small ball through an elevated hoop. Organized sports have been around for a long time.

2. Ask the class to discuss how the game four square is organized. If students do not have a good understanding of the game, they can research it online to prepare for the discussion. You can provide the categories for them if they get stuck (see http://www.squarefour.org/rules for more information).

3. As a class, discuss the following questions:
   ▸ How is four square organized? (Four people play at a time; they must hit the ball into measured squares.)
   ▸ What would happen if there were not rules to four square? (Players would not know which square to go to; they would not know how to win the game.)
   ▸ What are some ways you change four square when playing it out on the playground? (Students might have their own rule variations, such as the player in Square 1 having the ability to call certain rules.)
   ▸ Where do you see numbers and math in four square? (Players count the number of bounces, consider numbered squares, etc.)
   ▸ How does this math help to keep things organized? (Without it, players would not know who is winning or which square to go to.)

4. How could you add scoring to four square? (Players could keep track of how many times someone is in Square 1.)

5. What do you think might happen if you add more squares? (More people can play, but it might become confusing.)

6. What might happen if you make the squares bigger? (Players would have more room to move; the game would take up more space.)

7. How would you improve four square?

How Is Math Used in Sports?

1. Conduct a whole-class discussion about how math is used in various aspects of sports, such as scoring, time, dimensions of the playing field, and number of players.
2. Through discussion, have students generate as much information as they can about math in sports. You can divide them into groups by areas of interest in sports as well. You can have each group discuss or research examples and then present them to the class.
3. Students might discuss how football is scored (i.e., a touchdown is 6 points, a field goal is 3 points, etc.); how the game is timed (i.e., football is played in 15-minute quarters); the field (i.e., the rectangular field is 120 yards long and 53 1/3 yards wide and divided into 10-yard sections); the goal posts (i.e., they are 20 feet high and 18 1/2 feet wide); and the number of players (i.e., each team has 11 players on the field at a time).
4. Have students consider a wide range of sports, such as basketball, baseball, golf, tennis, and others with which they might be familiar.

HANDOUT 10.1

Practice Day

Directions: Work with a partner and clearly explain how your sport is played. You will also need to evaluate his or her sport. Use the following questions as you review your partner's sport.

1. Was the purpose of the sport clear?

2. How easy was it to see how the sport is played?

3. Could you understand how someone keeps score?

4. Did you get a clear picture of what the playing field looks like and how big it is?

5. Is it obvious how math is involved in the sport?

6. Did the rules make sense?

7. Were your questions answered?

Project 10: Construct and Explain Systems

PRODUCT RUBRIC

Everyone Is Playing It

	Sport	Math
Great	The rules of the sport are clearly laid out and easy for others to understand. The field the sport is played on is clearly demonstrated.	It is very clear how math is used in the sport. The math that is used in the sport makes sense and works mathematically.
Good	The rules of the sport are laid out but not always easy for others to understand. The field the sport is played on is demonstrated, but it is unclear in some ways.	One can see how math is used in the sport, but it is not always clear. The math that is used in the sport makes some sense but does not always work mathematically.
Needs improvement	The rules of the sport are not laid out clearly, making it difficult for others to understand how to play. The field the sport is played on is either not demonstrated or does not make sense.	It is unclear how math is used in the sport; it is never pointed out. The math that is used in the sport does not make sense and/or does not work mathematically.

DEVELOP YOUR OWN STEM PROJECTS

You can develop your own projects through the cycle depicted in Figure 7.

Define a Problem

Defining a problem can be handled in many different ways depending on the needs of the class and curriculum. One option is to base it on standards. Consider the Common Core Standards in math and language arts and the Next Generation Science Standards (NGSS). You could choose one of these as the basis of your problem. For example, here is a fifth-grade science standard from the NGSS:

> 5 ESS1-1 Support an argument that the apparent brightness of the sun and stars is due to their relative distances from the Earth.

One could easily construct a project from this problem, having students create a model that shows the relative distances of the sun and nearby stars. Students could even create a demonstration using flashlights that show the varying brightness of these objects as a result of distance.

You could also start with a national STEM learning goal, such as those that make up the structure of this book. Alternatively, you could consider 21st-century skills, such as collaboration and teamwork, creativity and imagination, critical thinking, problem solving, oral and written communication skills, social responsibility and citizenship, technology liter-

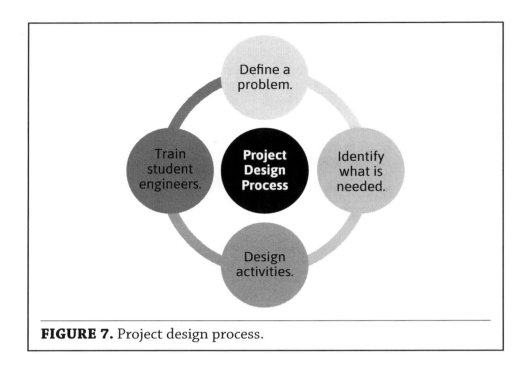

FIGURE 7. Project design process.

acy, and initiative. You could choose from one or more of these areas and develop a project. For example, if you wanted to focus on oral communication, you would have to design your project so that the final product required students to give an oral presentation to an authentic audience.

Yet another way to define a project is by exploring an authentic, real-world problem. Say there is an opioid problem in your school district, or your school is trying to figure out an effective way to run its recycling program. You could take either of these real-world situations and ask students to develop solutions.

Identify What Is Needed

The best way to figure out what is needed for a project is to start at the end. What do you want students to ideally turn in at the end of the project? What would this product look like or involve? Everything stems from this product, including the skills needed to accomplish it and the lessons you will need to teach in order for students to understand what they are doing. You want to have a general idea of what this product is going to look like, but you should not be so detailed that there is little student choice. As much as possible, you should provide students with choices in their products. This is where creativity comes into play as well as student empowerment. Providing students with choice engages them in the learning and will probably lead to a better quality product.

Once you have decided what the product is going to be, you can create the rubric that is going to evaluate it. This is where you set the performance criteria. This should be based on whatever way you chose to define the problem. For instance, if you are focusing on a very specific content standard, this should be reflected in the rubric. However, if you instead decided to focus on a 21st-century skill, the criteria for how to evaluate it need to be laid out in the rubric.

Design Activities

Once the product is put into place, you can backward build the rest of the project. I actually like to use a calendar like you see at the beginning of the projects in this book, putting the final product at the end and then building outward from there. For instance, if the project we were having students work on had a final product of a portfolio, I would have to consider what skills students need to employ and what information they need to find in order to complete the project.

If I were doing a project where students had to create a new mousetrap, one that did not harm the mouse, I would start with the completed mousetrap and then build backward from there. It might look like Figure 8.

This would be plotted out step by step until I reached the beginning of the project when it is being introduced to students. Then, I would go back and determine how much time I would need for each of step and plug the steps into a calendar. The final step is to reverse the order and make sure the project is following the engineering design process (see Figure 9).

Train Student Engineers

Now that you have the project figured out and the product determined, the most challenging part occurs. This is where the teacher has to train his or her student engineers. This means making sure that students have a firm understanding of the how the engineering design process works because it will be the backbone of every STEM project.

Part of this training may include how to work effectively in groups, because STEM projects often require students to have partners or multiple

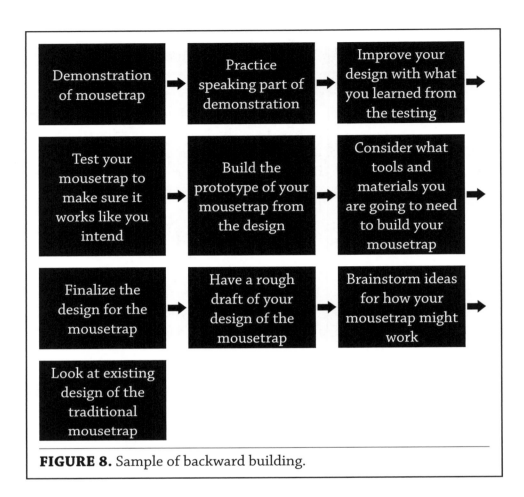

FIGURE 8. Sample of backward building.

team members. No matter students' age, it would be wrong to assume that they already know how to work with others successfully in the group setting. You will want to make sure to take some time to practice team-working skills and have guidelines for proper group behavior and expectations. You also need to determine ways to evaluate students not just on the overall product produced by the group, but also on what each student's contribution to that product was. If two students turn in the same work, but one contributed 90% of the work, it is not fair to give both an equal grade.

The role of the teacher shifts from being in front of the room, to acting as a coach from the side. It involves conversations with students and keen observation skills to determine when a group or student needs some help, and when you need to let them figure something out for themselves. Part of this is determining how to best use time and space—time in the form of opportunities for students to test and improve their results, and space in

DAY				
1 Introduce the project; review the design of the original mousetrap. *Ask.*	**2** Introduce students to the engineering design process. Allow them to begin brainstorming ideas. *Ask/Imagine.*	**3** Students begin to design their new mousetrap, conducting research to make sure it does not already exist. *Imagine/Plan.*	**4** Students finish designing their new mousetrap. *Plan.*	**5** Students create a list of materials needed to make the model of the mousetrap. *Plan.*
6 Students construct model of mousetrap. *Create.*	**7** Students construct model of mousetrap. *Create.*	**8** Students test mousetrap and make any improvements they think are needed. *Improve.*	**9** Students finish construction of model of mousetrap and test to make sure it works as intended. *Improve.*	**10** Students practice the speaking part of their demonstrations. *Improve.*
11 Students demonstrate their mousetraps.				

FIGURE 9. Sample project calendar. Adapted from *10 Performance-Based Projects for the Science Classroom* (p. 99), by T. Stanley, 2017, Waco, TX: Prufrock Press. Copyright 2017 by Prufrock Press. Adapted with permission.

the form of learning without interference of the teacher. The best learning is discovery learning, which, as a teacher, means sometimes figuring out how to get out of students' way.

Your role is to manage the project, not determine its path. You will need to figure out what skills students might need to have before they can be successful. For instance, if the project calls for students to conduct interviews, do they have the knowledge of how to do these, or are there tips and guidelines you can point them to in order to make their chances for meaningful success that much greater? Keep in mind that most of the heavy lifting should be done by the students.

REFERENCES

Advancement Courses. (2015). *The engineering design process: The 4 key steps to STEM teaching and learning* [Web log post]. Retrieved from https://www.advancementcourses.com/blog/the-engineering-design-process-the-4-key-steps-to-stem-teaching-and-learning

Boaler, J. (2002). Learning from teaching: Exploring the relationship between reform curriculum and equity. *Journal for Research in Mathematics Education, 33,* 239–258.

Buck Institute for Education. (n.d.). *Why PBL?* Retrieved from https://www.bie.org/about/why_pbl

Center for Writers. (n.d.). *Writing about art.* Retrieved from http://www.cameron.edu/~carolynk/aboutart.html

Condliffe, B. (2017). *Project-based learning: A literature review* [Working paper]. New York, NY: MDRC.

Creative Learning Exchange. (2016). *Using system dynamics and systems thinking (SD/ST) tools and learning strategies to build science, technology, engineering, and math excellence.* Retrieved from http://www.clexchange.org/curriculum/standards/stem.asp

Deitering, S. (2016). *Is project based learning a more effective way of teaching than traditional teaching?* (Master's thesis, Northwester College, Orange, City IA). Retrieved from https://nwcommons.nwciowa.edu/education_masters/12

Digital Harbor Foundation. (2018). *Project: Art bots.* Retrieved from https://blueprint.digitalharbor.org/sample-projects/art-bots

Dintersmith, T., & Whiteley, G. (2015). *Most likely to succeed* [Motion picture]. United States: One Potato Productions.

Engineering is Elementary. (2018). *The engineering design process*. Retrieved from https://www.eie.org/overview/engineering-design-process

Graduate Management Admission Council. (2018). *Employers seek communication skills in new hires*. Retrieved from https://www.mba.com/mbas-and-business-masters/articles/your-career-path/employers-seek-communications-skills

International Technology and Engineering Educators Association. (2016). *About*. Retrieved from https://www.iteea.org/About.aspx

Mathison, S., & Feeman, M. (1997). *The logic of interdisciplinary studies*. Presented at the Annual Meeting of the American Educational Research Association, Chicago, IL.

Menzies, V., Hewitt, C., Kokotsaki, D., Collyer, C., & Wiggins, A. (2016). *Project-based learning: Evaluation report and executive summary*. London, England: Education Endowment Foundation.

Partnership for 21st Century Skills. (2016). *P21 framework definitions*. Washington, DC: Author.

Scholastic. (n.d.). *Building abstract thinking through math*. Retrieved from https://www.scholastic.com/teachers/articles/teaching-content/building-abstract-thinking-through-math

Stanley, T. (2015). *Creating life-long learners: Using project-based management to teach 21st century skills*. Thousand Oaks, CA: Corwin.

Stanley, T. (2017). *10 performance-based projects for the science classroom*. Waco, TX: Prufrock Press.

Stanley, T. (2018). *When smart kids underachieve in school: Practical solutions for teachers*. Waco, TX: Prufrock Press.

Thomas, J. W. (2000). *A review of research on project-based learning*. San Rafael, CA: Autodesk Foundation.

ABOUT THE AUTHOR

Todd Stanley is author of many teacher education books, including *Project-Based Learning for Gifted Students: A Handbook for the 21st-Century Classroom* and *Performance-Based Assessment for 21st-Century Skills*. He was a classroom teacher for 18 years, teaching students as young as second graders and as old as high school seniors, and was a National Board Certified teacher. He helped create a gifted academy for grades 5–8, which employs inquiry-based learning, project-based learning, and performance-based assessment. He is currently the gifted services coordinator for Pickerington Local School District in Ohio, where he lives with his wife, Nicki, and two daughters, Anna and Abby. You can follow him on Twitter @the_gifted_guy or visit his website at https://www.thegiftedguy.com.

NEXT GENERATION SCIENCE STANDARDS ALIGNMENT

Project	Next Generation Science Standards
Project 1	K-2-ETS1-1. Ask questions, make observations, and gather information about a situation people want to change to define a simple problem that can be solved through the development of a new or improved object or tool.
	K-2-ETS1-2. Develop a simple sketch, drawing, or physical model to illustrate how the shape of an object helps it function as needed to solve a given problem.
Project 2	K-2-ETS1-1. Ask questions, make observations, and gather information about a situation people want to change to define a simple problem that can be solved through the development of a new or improved object or tool.
	K-2-ETS1-2. Develop a simple sketch, drawing, or physical model to illustrate how the shape of an object helps it function as needed to solve a given problem.
Project 3	K-2-ETS1-3. Analyze data from tests of two objects designed to solve the same problem to compare the strengths and weaknesses of how each performs.

Project	Next Generation Science Standards
Project 4	K-ESS3-3. Communicate solutions that will reduce the impact of humans on the land, water, air, and/or other living things in the local environment.
	K-2-ETS1-2. Develop a simple sketch, drawing, or physical model to illustrate how the shape of an object helps it function as needed to solve a given problem.
Project 7	K-2-ETS1-1. Ask questions, make observations, and gather information about a situation people want to change to define a simple problem that can be solved through the development of a new or improved object or tool.
	K-2-ETS1-2. Develop a simple sketch, drawing, or physical model to illustrate how the shape of an object helps it function as needed to solve a given problem.
	K-2-ETS1-3. Analyze data from tests of two objects designed to solve the same problem to compare the strengths and weaknesses of how each performs.
Project 8	K-ESS2-1. Use and share observations of local weather conditions to describe patterns over time.
Project 9	K-2-ETS1-1. Ask questions, make observations, and gather information about a situation people want to change to define a simple problem that can be solved through the development of a new or improved object or tool.
	K-2-ETS1-2. Develop a simple sketch, drawing, or physical model to illustrate how the shape of an object helps it function as needed to solve a given problem.

COMMON CORE STATE STANDARDS ALIGNMENT

Project	Subject	Standards
Project 1	ELA	SL.K.1 Participate in collaborative conversations with diverse partners about kindergarten topics and texts with peers and adults in small and larger groups.
		SL.K.2 Confirm understanding of a text read aloud or information presented orally or through other media by asking and answering questions about key details and requesting clarification if something is not understood.
		SL.K.3 Ask and answer questions in order to seek help, get information, or clarify something that is not understood.
		SL.K.4 Describe familiar people, places, things, and events and, with prompting and support, provide additional detail.
		SL.K.5 Add drawings or other visual displays to descriptions as desired to provide additional detail.
		SL.K.6 Speak audibly and express thoughts, feelings, and ideas clearly.

Project	Subject	Standards
Project 1, *continued*	ELA, *continued*	L.K.1 Demonstrate command of the conventions of standard English grammar and usage when writing or speaking.
		L.K.6 Use words and phrases acquired through conversations, reading and being read to, and responding to texts.
		SL.1.1 Participate in collaborative conversations with diverse partners about grade 1 topics and texts with peers and adults in small and larger groups.
		SL.1.2 Ask and answer questions about key details in a text read aloud or information presented orally or through other media.
		SL.1.3 Ask and answer questions about what a speaker says in order to gather additional information or clarify something that is not understood.
		SL.1.4 Describe people, places, things, and events with relevant details, expressing ideas and feelings clearly.
		SL.1.5 Add drawings or other visual displays to descriptions when appropriate to clarify ideas, thoughts, and feelings.
		SL.1.6 Produce complete sentences when appropriate to task and situation.
		L.1.1 Demonstrate command of the conventions of standard English grammar and usage when writing or speaking.
		L.1.6 Use words and phrases acquired through conversations, reading and being read to, and responding to texts, including using frequently occurring conjunctions to signal simple relationships (e.g., because).

Project	Subject	Standards
Project 2	ELA	RF.K.3 Know and apply grade-level phonics and word analysis skills in decoding words.
		RF.K.4 Read emergent-reader texts with purpose and understanding.
		W.K.3 Use a combination of drawing, dictating, and writing to narrate a single event or several loosely linked events, tell about the events in the order in which they occurred, and provide a reaction to what happened.
		SL.K.1 Participate in collaborative conversations with diverse partners about kindergarten topics and texts with peers and adults in small and larger groups.
		SL.K.2 Confirm understanding of a text read aloud or information presented orally or through other media by asking and answering questions about key details and requesting clarification if something is not understood.
		SL.K.3 Ask and answer questions in order to seek help, get information, or clarify something that is not understood.
		SL.K.6 Speak audibly and express thoughts, feelings, and ideas clearly.
		RF.1.3 Know and apply grade-level phonics and word analysis skills in decoding words.
		RF.1.4 Read with sufficient accuracy and fluency to support comprehension.
		W.1.3 Write narratives in which they recount two or more appropriately sequenced events, include some details regarding what happened, use temporal words to signal event order, and provide some sense of closure.
		SL.1.1 Participate in collaborative conversations with diverse partners about grade 1 topics and texts with peers and adults in small and larger groups.

Project	Subject	Standards
Project 2, *continued*	ELA, *continued*	SL.1.3 Ask and answer questions about what a speaker says in order to gather additional information or clarify something that is not understood.
		SL.1.6 Produce complete sentences when appropriate to task and situation.
Project 3	ELA	RL.K.1 With prompting and support, ask and answer questions about key details in a text.
		SL.K.1 Participate in collaborative conversations with diverse partners about kindergarten topics and texts with peers and adults in small and larger groups.
		SL.K.2 Confirm understanding of a text read aloud or information presented orally or through other media by asking and answering questions about key details and requesting clarification if something is not understood.
		SL.K.3 Ask and answer questions in order to seek help, get information, or clarify something that is not understood.
		SL.K.4 Describe familiar people, places, things, and events and, with prompting and support, provide additional detail.
		SL.K.6 Speak audibly and express thoughts, feelings, and ideas clearly.
		RL.1.1 Ask and answer questions about key details in a text.
		RL.1.4 Identify words and phrases in stories or poems that suggest feelings or appeal to the senses.
		RL.1.10 With prompting and support, read prose and poetry of appropriate complexity for grade 1.
		SL.1.1 Participate in collaborative conversations with diverse partners about grade 1 topics and texts with peers and adults in small and larger groups.

Project	Subject	Standards
Project 3, continued	ELA, continued	SL.1.2 Ask and answer questions about key details in a text read aloud or information presented orally or through other media.
		SL.1.3 Ask and answer questions about what a speaker says in order to gather additional information or clarify something that is not understood.
		SL.1.4 Describe people, places, things, and events with relevant details, expressing ideas and feelings clearly.
		SL.1.6 Produce complete sentences when appropriate to task and situation.
	Math	K.CC.A Know number names and the count sequence.
		K.MD.B.3 Classify objects into given categories; count the numbers of objects in each category and sort the categories by count.
		1.NBT.A Extend the counting sequence.
		1.MD.C.4 Organize, represent, and interpret data with up to three categories; ask and answer questions about the total number of data points, how many in each category, and how many more or less are in one category than in another.
Project 4	ELA	W.K.2 Use a combination of drawing, dictating, and writing to compose informative/explanatory texts in which they name what they are writing about and supply some information about the topic.
		SL.K.1 Participate in collaborative conversations with diverse partners about kindergarten topics and texts with peers and adults in small and larger groups.

Project	Subject	Standards
Project 4, *continued*	ELA, *continued*	SL.K.2 Confirm understanding of a text read aloud or information presented orally or through other media by asking and answering questions about key details and requesting clarification if something is not understood.
		SL.K.3 Ask and answer questions in order to seek help, get information, or clarify something that is not understood.
		SL.1.1 Participate in collaborative conversations with diverse partners about grade 1 topics and texts with peers and adults in small and larger groups.
		SL.1.2 Ask and answer questions about key details in a text read aloud or information presented orally or through other media.
		SL.1.3 Ask and answer questions about what a speaker says in order to gather additional information or clarify something that is not understood.
Project 5	ELA	W.K.2 Use a combination of drawing, dictating, and writing to compose informative/explanatory texts in which they name what they are writing about and supply some information about the topic.
		W.1.2 Write informative/explanatory texts in which they name a topic, supply some facts about the topic, and provide some sense of closure.
	Math	*Note.* Standards for this project vary based on how students develop and represent their codes.
Project 6	ELA	SL.K.1 Participate in collaborative conversations with diverse partners about kindergarten topics and texts with peers and adults in small and larger groups.

Project	Subject	Standards
Project 6, *continued*	ELA, *continued*	SL.K.2 Confirm understanding of a text read aloud or information presented orally or through other media by asking and answering questions about key details and requesting clarification if something is not understood.
		SL.K.3 Ask and answer questions in order to seek help, get information, or clarify something that is not understood.
		SL.K.4 Describe familiar people, places, things, and events and, with prompting and support, provide additional detail.
		SL.K.6 Speak audibly and express thoughts, feelings, and ideas clearly.
		SL.1.1 Participate in collaborative conversations with diverse partners about grade 1 topics and texts with peers and adults in small and larger groups.
		SL.1.2 Ask and answer questions about key details in a text read aloud or information presented orally or through other media.
		SL.1.3 Ask and answer questions about what a speaker says in order to gather additional information or clarify something that is not understood.
		SL.1.4 Describe people, places, things, and events with relevant details, expressing ideas and feelings clearly.
		SL.1.6 Produce complete sentences when appropriate to task and situation.
Project 7	ELA	SL.K.1 Participate in collaborative conversations with diverse partners about kindergarten topics and texts with peers and adults in small and larger groups.

Project	Subject	Standards
Project 7, *continued*	ELA, *continued*	SL.K.2 Confirm understanding of a text read aloud or information presented orally or through other media by asking and answering questions about key details and requesting clarification if something is not understood.
		SL.1.1 Participate in collaborative conversations with diverse partners about grade 1 topics and texts with peers and adults in small and larger groups.
		SL.1.2 Ask and answer questions about key details in a text read aloud or information presented orally or through other media.
	Math	K.MD.A Describe and compare measurable attributes.
		1.MD.A Measure lengths indirectly and by iterating length units.
		1.MD.C Represent and interpret data.
		2.MD.A Measure and estimate lengths in standard units.
Project 8	ELA	W.K.2 Use a combination of drawing, dictating, and writing to compose informative/explanatory texts in which they name what they are writing about and supply some information about the topic.
		W.K.3 Use a combination of drawing, dictating, and writing to narrate a single event or several loosely linked events, tell about the events in the order in which they occurred, and provide a reaction to what happened.
		W.K.8 With guidance and support from adults, recall information from experiences or gather information from provided sources to answer a question.
		SL.K.1 Participate in collaborative conversations with diverse partners about kindergarten topics and texts with peers and adults in small and larger groups.

Project	Subject	Standards
Project 8, *continued*	ELA, *continued*	SL.K.2 Confirm understanding of a text read aloud or information presented orally or through other media by asking and answering questions about key details and requesting clarification if something is not understood.
		W.1.2 Write informative/explanatory texts in which they name a topic, supply some facts about the topic, and provide some sense of closure.
		W.1.3 Write narratives in which they recount two or more appropriately sequenced events, include some details regarding what happened, use temporal words to signal event order, and provide some sense of closure.
		W.1.5 With guidance and support from adults, focus on a topic, respond to questions and suggestions from peers, and add details to strengthen writing as needed.
		W.1.8 With guidance and support from adults, recall information from experiences or gather information from provided sources to answer a question.
		SL.1.1 Participate in collaborative conversations with diverse partners about grade 1 topics and texts with peers and adults in small and larger groups.
		SL.1.2 Ask and answer questions about key details in a text read aloud or information presented orally or through other media.
Project 9	ELA	SL.K.1 Participate in collaborative conversations with diverse partners about kindergarten topics and texts with peers and adults in small and larger groups.
		SL.K.2 Confirm understanding of a text read aloud or information presented orally or through other media by asking and answering questions about key details and requesting clarification if something is not understood.

Project	Subject	Standards
Project 9, *continued*	ELA, *continued*	SL.K.3 Ask and answer questions in order to seek help, get information, or clarify something that is not understood.
		SL.K.4 Describe familiar people, places, things, and events and, with prompting and support, provide additional detail.
		SL.K.6 Speak audibly and express thoughts, feelings, and ideas clearly.
		SL.1.1 Participate in collaborative conversations with diverse partners about grade 1 topics and texts with peers and adults in small and larger groups.
		SL.1.2 Ask and answer questions about key details in a text read aloud or information presented orally or through other media.
		SL.1.3 Ask and answer questions about what a speaker says in order to gather additional information or clarify something that is not understood.
		SL.1.4 Describe people, places, things, and events with relevant details, expressing ideas and feelings clearly.
		SL.1.6 Produce complete sentences when appropriate to task and situation.
Project 10	Math	K.CC.A Know number names and the count sequence.
		K.OA.A Understand addition, and understand subtraction.
		K.MD.A Describe and compare measurable attributes.
		K.G.A Identify and describe shapes.
		K.G.B Analyze, compare, create, and compose shapes.
		1.OA.A Represent and solve problems involving addition and subtraction.

Project	Subject	Standards
Project 10, *continued*	Math, *continued*	1.OA.B Understand and apply properties of operations and the relationship between addition and subtraction.
		1.MD.A Measure lengths indirectly and by iterating length units.
		1.MD.C Represent and interpret data.
		2.MD.A Measure and estimate lengths in standard units.
		1.G.A Reason with shapes and their attributes